"Digital Art Masters is a great album filled not only with eye candy imagery, but also with a technical and creative knowledge base that every aspiring artist should read. Techniques, methodology and tips from industry professionals found in the book are truly useful and sometimes mind opening for both beginner and veteran CG artist alike. From pure 2D Photoshop painting, through to photo collages and 3D rendered images enhanced with compositing tools, this book is a valuable addition to any modern professional's library."

GRZEGORZ JONKAJTYS
HTTP://WWW.3DLUVR.COM/JONKAJTYS

"I highly recommend Digital Art Masters for all artists. This book meticulously records the artists' inner thoughts, personal techniques and creative processes. The comprehensive explanations alongside detailed breakdown progress images are great learning tools for both students and professionals."

SZE JONES
HTTP://SZEJONES.COM

"Digital Art Masters is getting better and better at showcasing some of today's best digital artists. The way the book shows the processes of achieving great pictures provides a good opportunity to learn from these artists, and keeps you challenged in your own Art."

RAPHAEL LACOSTE
HTTP://WWW.RAPHAEL-LACOSTE.COM

"The Digital Art Masters is a collection of truly extraordinary talents and their captivating imagery. Filled with creative and practical techniques, this insightful glance into such remarkable minds makes this a must have for every artist."

JULIANNA KOLAKIS
HTTP://WWW.KOLAKISART.COM

"Digital Art Masters is a dazzling line up of the industry's digital art elite. It is exceedingly inspiring, not only because of the top notch art shown in the book, but the useful tips and thoughts that the artists share in their articles make it a must-have for every aspiring digital artist."

MICHAEL KUTSCHE
HTTP://WWW.MISTERMK.DE/

DIGITAL ART MASTERS
: VOLUME 4

FEATURED ARTISTS

Alexey Kashpersky

Andrée Wallin

Andrei Kashkin

Andrew Hickinbottom

Andrius Balciunas

Andrzej Sykut

Blaz Porenta

Bradford Rigney

Bruno Melo de Souza

Cesar Martinez Alvaro

Craig Sellars

Daarken

Daniel Lieske

Denis C. Feliz

Eduardo Peña

Fabricio Moraes

Gerhard Mozsi

Gregory Callahan

Hao Ai Qiang

Iker Cortázar

James Paick

Jelmer Boskma

Jonathan Simard

Kekai Kotaki

Leonid Kozienko

Loïc e338 Zimmermann

Maciej Kuciara

Marc Brunet

Marek Denko

Marek Okoń

Martin Carlsson

Michal Kwolek

Nicholas Miles

Nykolai Aleksander

Piotr Luziński

Roberto F · Castro

Rudolf Herczog

Ryohei Hase

Sarel Theron

Sebastien Haure

Sönke Maeter

Stefan Morrell

Thibaut Milville

Till Nowak

Titus Lunter

Tomáš Král

Tomáš Müller

Viktor Fretyán

Viktor Titov

Weiye Yin

DIGITAL ART MASTERS
: VOLUME 4

3DTOTAL.COM LTD

Routledge
Taylor & Francis Group

LONDON AND NEW YORK

First published 2009 by Focal Press

Published 2017 by Routledge
2 Park Square, Milton Park, Abingdon, Oxon OX14 4RN
711 Third Avenue, New York, NY 10017, USA

First issued in hardback 2017

Routledge is an imprint of the Taylor & Francis Group, an informa business

Notices

Practitioners and researchers must always rely on their own experience and
knowledge in evaluating and using any information, methods, compounds, or
experiments described herein. In using such information or methods they should
be mindful of their own safety and the safety of others, including parties for whom
they have a professional responsibility.

To the fullest extent of the law, neither the Publisher nor the authors,
contributors, or editors, assume any liability for any injury and/or damage to
persons or property as a matter of products liability, negligence or otherwise, or
from any use or operation of any methods, products, instructions, or ideas
contained in the material herein.

Library of Congress Control Number: 2009901729

British Library Cataloguing in Publication Data
Digital Art Masters.
Volume 4.
1. Digital Art.
I. 3DTotal.com (Firm)
776' .0922-dc22

ISBN 13: 978-1-138-41781-6 (hbk)
ISBN 13: 978-0-240-52170-1 (pbk)

CONTENTS

CONTENTS

 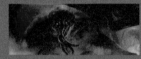

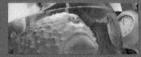 

DIGITAL ART MASTERS

: VOLUME 4

COMPILED BY THE 3DTOTAL TEAM

INTRODUCTION

The Digital Art Masters series was born from a realization that there was missing from the market something that showcased not only high quality gallery images, but also shared the thought processes and creation techniques behind such stunning imagery. Since Volume 1 we have seen a huge growth in the popularity of this series, which has been demonstrated not only in the sales of the books, but also in the support from the CG community and contributing artists. We had over a staggering 1100 art submissions for this fourth volume in the series – we could have very easily created a book at least five times the size of the one you are holding right now with images all of the quality that you will see as you make your way through the following pages.

These books are collaborations; they are the product of many months of labor and many nights and weekends spent, not in the sun, but at a computer desk behind a glowing screen. Each volume of the DAM series is an emotional rollercoaster – from the very moment that I email artists to confirm receipt of their submissions, to the judging process with the 3DTotal team and our guest judges, through the ups and downs of the content creation to the final moments before sending the book to print. I would love to be able to measure the amount of energy that goes into one of our volumes – not only from the 3DTotal team but the physical and mental energy that each artist devotes and contributes. The hours

TOM GREENWAY

LYNETTE CLEE

CHRIS PERRINS

RICHARD TILBURY

that the artists give to us are priceless, and I never fail to be moved by the sheer warmth of the CG community; the way in which groups of artists from all corners of the globe will come together to create something beautiful, such as this fourth volume in our DAM series. This year in fact we again boast artists from Africa, Asia, Australia/Oceania, Europe, North America and South America, making this volume yet another diverse collection of talents from, quite literally, all around the world.

The CG community is buzzing greater than ever with the most wonderful artwork ever being created, making our task in the judging process as painful as it possibly could be when having to make a decision to take one image over another. As this year's guest judges found, the task is not an enviable one, but at the same time you could not help but be overwhelmed and feel honored by the sight of an entire room literally filled wall to wall with the most gorgeous collection of work you could hope to see in one place at one time. Just fifty of those images are here today in this collection, making this just a tiny taste of what the CG community has to offer. The articles that you'll find as you move through the book have been created by artists, for artists. We are the mere compilers of the stunning artwork and write-ups you're about to see and read, and we produce these books to give the artists within these pages the exposure and merit that they deserve, for they are each in their own right a Master of their digital art. And it is on this note that I'd like to thank each and every contributor to this volume of the DAM series: the artists, the translators, the guest judges, the friends and families who have supported the artists through their late nights and weekends at their computers, as well as the publishers who have made Volume 4 possible. Finally, we thank you, the reader, for investing in the DAM series; we hope you'll thoroughly enjoy this latest offering and that it may lead to the creation of your very own digital art masterpiece.

LYNETTE CLEE
CONTENT MANAGER, 3DTOTAL

CAPSULA © EDUARDO PEÑA

FOREWORD

I remember it like it was yesterday: my first year at university, I had no idea about my future, and then I stumbled across the mind-blowing works of an illustrator whilst shuffling through the pages of an art magazine. From that very moment, I realized what I wanted to do with my future. The images adorning the pages of the magazine changed the flow of my life; my passion for digital art had started to develop. I discovered that the possibilities and things that could be achieved were almost endless – and without any further thinking, I leapt into the "endless" world of digital art ...

After first deciding to be an illustrator, I would never have guessed that one day someone would spread countless numbers of awesome artworks in front of me and ask me to choose the very best of them. So when the 3DTotal staff asked me to help them out with the judging process of this fourth volume of the Digital Art Masters series, I was really honored, but at the same time I had the nagging feeling that I was about to get myself into a really tough situation ... When the judging day finally arrived, we laid out all of the prints on the ground, and I realized that I was right about my initial concerns – we were choosing the best of the best! As an artist, it's not difficult for me to draw or to paint, but it soon turned out that it was pretty tough for me to choose from the awesome artworks that have been created by so many freakishly talented artists – all who share the same passion as me.

The book you're holding right now is the fruit of many tough moments, plenty of sweat, battles of indecision and many, many cups of coffee.

The world of digital art is so endless that it's very hard not to get lost in it. Someone who is just beginning needs to figure out what to do first, but the internet has almost turned into a tutorial garbage dump. So at this point, the Digital Art Masters series takes its place on the shelf of "must have" classic art books for artists and art enthusiasts alike. This fourth volume of the series is a particular reference to where digital art has come to today.

I'm pretty sure that most people who gaze at the pages of this book will have similar feelings to mine when I first looked at that art magazine many years back. Perhaps there will even be some confused students, curious art lovers and even potential artists who haven't yet discovered their talents but will somehow obtain this book, and whilst looking through the images and articles they will unconsciously be opening a fresh page in a new chapter of their lives.

I congratulate the 3DTotal team and Focal Press for getting this book together and for supporting the world of digital art. Through these efforts, many new artists will reveal and push the limits of digital art. So, if your coffee is ready, prepare yourself to turn the first page of this new visual adventure.

EMRAH ELMASLI
http://www.emrahelmasli.com | hello@emrahelmasli.com

THE VILLAGE
BY ANDRÉE WALLIN

SOFTWARE USED: Photoshop CS3

INTRODUCTION

The Village was created as a concept for a friend and colleague of mine. He was in the making of a World War II tank and needed an environment to place it in, so he asked if I could create something for him. I had recently looked at some of John Wallin's work on *Gears of War* and I had fallen in love with his ability to create winter scenes with a very loose and yet clean style. I really wanted to try something similar with this particular scene, and my goal was to create an environment that had been touched by war, but also something colorful and with a nice feeling of serenity to it, since most WWII pieces are very desaturated, gritty and dark.

WORKFLOW

I chose to do a "matte painting concept", which means working with real photos but still keeping it pretty rough around the edges to save some time. I found a really

Fig.01

good photograph taken by Paul Stevenson that I used as a plate (**Fig.01**), and started by blocking out the changes I wanted to make to the composition (**Fig.02**).

Since the original photo is sepia toned, I created a few layers with mainly blue and orange colors and played around with the blending modes until it started to look

Fig.02

interesting. I also started painting some snow, looking for some nice values (**Fig.03**). After that I copied and pasted some parts of the image and used the Warp tool to reshape them; for example, the road was too straight for my taste, so I made it a little curvier (**Fig.04**). The Warp tool is really helpful and I use it frequently.

After that I continued working on the snow and the little town square in the middle (**Fig.05**). I kept it very loose with a simple round Photoshop brush. There was no need for custom brushes on this one – I actually rarely use custom brushes for my concepts. Since I used a plate for this one I didn't have to spend that much time on the composition and could go straight to figuring out the lighting, which I think is the best part of this image. I was actually just playing around with a gradient layer set to Screen that made the top of the buildings highlighted, creating the feel of an early evening. I really liked it,

Fig.03

Fig.04

Fig.06

Fig.05

so from then on it was just a matter of finding the right values for the shadowed areas and starting work on the details.

If I'm working on a high end render or a detailed matte painting I always use tons of layers, but when I have a tight deadline, and if I'm doing a concept like this one (one day), I never use more than four or five layers at once. I flatten the image every now and then throughout the process, just to force myself not to go to crazy on the details and to keep it simple and efficient. As you can see, the brushstrokes are very rough in some places; it's just a matter of fooling the eye to make it look detailed (**Fig.06 – 07**).

I was starting to see the end at this stage (**Fig.08**), basically just working up the details from here on in. The big advantage of working with a winter scene like this one is that you don't have to worry that much about tons of different values; once you find the right tone for the snow you can use it pretty much over the entire scene. And as you can see, I found this pretty early in the process. I picked out two very similar values to work with, and for the final image I also integrated a few photos of real snow (taken by me) (**Fig.09a – b**), along with a great image that I found on cgtextures.com for the sky, to give the image a more authentic effect (**Fig.10**).

Fig.07

Fig.08

© ANDRÉE WALLIN
Fig.09a

© ANDRÉE WALLIN
Fig.09b

CONCLUSION

This was a really fun concept for me to do: I found a good plate rather quickly, the process was smooth, and the result pretty much what I aimed for. There's something about post apocalyptic sceneries that really speaks to me. I love the serenity and the beauty of destroyed civilizations. Everything looks so peaceful and calm, and that's what I hope people will feel when they look at *The Village*.

Fig.10

© Andree Wallin, Realtime UK

© Andree Wallin

© Andree Wallin

© Andree Wallin

LONELY DRIVER
BY ANDREI KASHKIN

SOFTWARE USED: 3d Studio Max, V-Ray, Vue and Photoshop

INTRODUCTION

Lonely Driver was a personal project that became a great challenge for me, because I was using some of the programs and techniques for the very first time. The idea of creating a highly detailed image of a car on a road had been in my mind for a long time, but I just wasn't sure how to make the concept look good … After watching a movie where the main character was rushing down the highway in rainy weather, I finally felt inspired; I could feel the loneliness of the character at the time, and I understood at that moment that I wanted to create the same feelings in my own artwork.

I really enjoyed making experiments for this project, and in total I spent about two months of my free time on it. To kick the project off, I started by searching for references on the internet. It was important to find not

© Andrei Kashkin

© iStockphoto.com/Alexander Hafemann (Mlenny)

Fig.01a

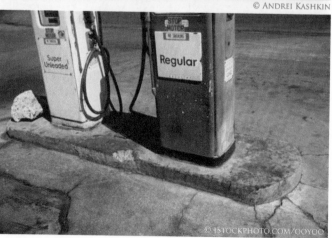

© iStockphoto.com/ooyoo

Fig.01b

only photos of the desert, which I wanted to use in order to underline the feelings of emptiness and loneliness, but also to find images of a certain style. In the end, I decided to go with a different kind of scene – American grassland with an old 1980s gas station, with the 1970 Dodge Challenger car parked in front of it (**Fig.01a – b**).

MODELING

I started by modeling the basic objects in low quality, in order to gauge the necessary composition early on. Almost all of the objects in the scene were made from primitives that were converted into editable polygons and then edited. Once objects displayed the correct geometrical form and looked natural, I applied chamfers along their corners and either altered the vertices manually or by way of the Noise modifier. The car, as the center of the composition, was modeled in high detail (**Fig.02**).

Bushes were created using Onyx Tree Storm. I made some different types of bushes, changing the parameters of the standard presets. I also created the dried-up stalks of the grass here, too, and for the grass arrangement I used the Adv Painter Script with different options for rotate, inclination and scale. Some kinds of grass were also modeled manually and multiplied using the Scatter function (Compound object). To place the grass in the cracks of the asphalt, I drew splines on the displacement structure; these splines were then scattered (**Fig.03**).

The lawn in the distance was exported from Vue and multiplied with the Adv Painter script.

CAMERA

I used a VRay Physical Camera with 35 FOV. Upon its integration into the scene I tried to use the principles of

Fig.02

Fig.03

Fig.04

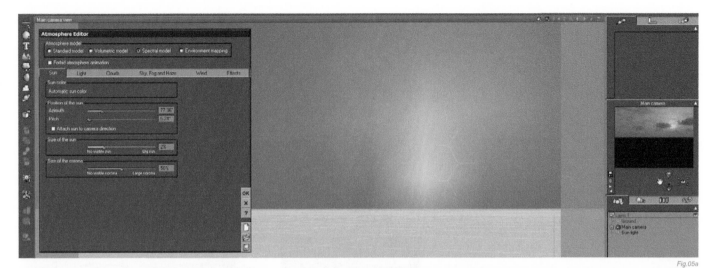

Fig.05a

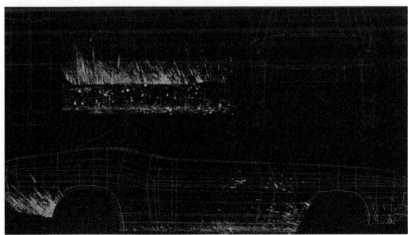

Fig.05b

classic photography to capture my image, in order to achieve a dramatic shot with good composition (**Fig.04**).

LIGHTING

For me, the lighting setup was a very important part of the creation process of this work. With well-established lighting it is possible to achieve tremendous results. I used the sky's HDR, which was made in Vue (**Fig.05a – b**); it worked well as the intensity of illumination and its color depended on a sky texture. I therefore got rid of any wrong adjustment sources of illumination and the rendered picture looks natural as a result. I wanted the sun to be behind the clouds, close to the horizon line in order that the scene received illumination with soft shadows; all parameters were set in the Atmosphere Editor. When I achieved some nice results, I rendered the sky in an HDR file. I also used additional light sources: a VRay Light plane in the building and a VRay Light dome for the whole scene (this way it was possible to supervise the brightness of the scene at invariable brightness levels of the sky).

SPECULAR   DIFFUSE

Fig.06a

SHADERS & TEXTURES

For the texture creation I used photos from the internet and dirt masks from the Total Textures collections. The majority of the materials were made as VRayMtl shaders with diffuse, bump and reflection maps. Sometimes for the bump maps I used noise and smoke maps or

Fig.06b

a combination in a mixed map. You can see some examples in **Fig.06a – c**. It was necessary to give special attention to the wet asphalt, as there were two types used in the scene (**Fig.07**). As a basis I took materials from vraymaterials.de, but they did need to be altered in order for me to achieve the necessary results.

Cracks on the road were made by displacing textures with cracks. Plants were textured with procedural materials (in the diffuse maps there was a noise map with different colors of grass), but because each type of grass had a separate material, it created a realistic-looking result.

PARTICLES

The weather was of great importance in terms of capturing the mood of the image. You can see the fog and the rain which were made using particle flow (**Fig.08**); a drip system was bound with gravitation and wind force. For the splash deflector I used the UOmniFlect deflector containing the objects in the scene (because of the miscalculation of collisions I needed lots of system resources and a lot of time, and therefore the objects that were low poly, along with the small objects, including the grass, were not involved) (**Fig.09**). The rain consisted of about 6000 droplets, which were rendered as spheres with motion blur. The fog was also made with particle flow with wind force, and was rendered with the AfterBurn plugin. The scene was rendered in separate layers (this way was faster, plus it was possible to regulate the color parameters individually).

Fig.06c

Fig.07

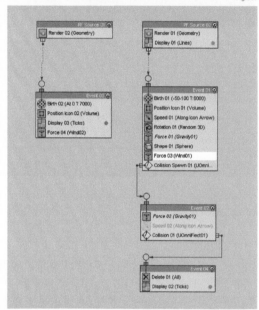

Fig.08

Fig.09

RENDERING & POST-PRODUCTION

The scene was rendered using V-Ray, without GI in order to reduce the render time and PC resources. Standard options were used; I only changed anti-aliasing on Catmull-Rom and in the adaptive subdivision window image sampler, and I changed the value of Clr tresh to 0,0.

Post-processing work would have been easy in any program; for this image I used Photoshop. I changed the brightness/contrast, color balance and saturation for each layer, and then merged it with different opacity and blending parameters (**Fig.10a – c**).

CONCLUSION

The searching of references is a very important stage for me in which I define the details and solve how the final image will look. Without sketches, I start work from rough modeling through to the details, and then I pass to the lighting setup and finally the shading. In the course of creating a work I experiment, using different programs and working methods to achieve good results and get lots of experience. High scene detailing allows you to concentrate on the idea and the mood, and not detract from the quality of the work.

Fig.10a

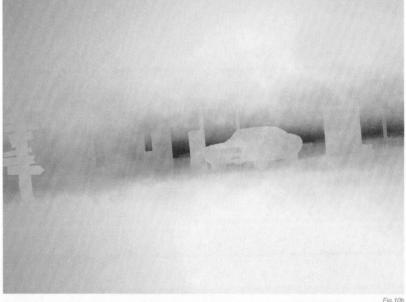
Fig.10b

Fig.10c

ARTIST PORTFOLIO

CHURCH OF CALATRAVAS
BY CESAR MARTINEZ ALVARO

SOFTWARE USED: 3d Studio Max, Photoshop and Combustion

INTRODUCTION

The title of this personal work is *Church of Calatravas*, which is an image based on one of the most famous streets in Madrid, La Gran Via. I like the center of Madrid – the architecture, the classic buildings – it's the perfect city upon which to create a 3D image. In my case I enjoy creating 3D environments and up until this point had not made any images based on real environments, so I selected the scene after seeing a photo published in a newspaper. The article commented on the restoration works on the Church of Calatravas. I knew Alcala Street, but I did not remember this building, which is why I like Madrid – always full of surprises.

I spent more or less three months of my free time completing the scene, from the searching of references right through to the post-production work – through the modeling, texturing, shading, lighting, and rendering. A lot of time was dedicated to this work, but I really enjoyed each and every step of the process.

REFERENCES

The composition of the scene is based on something real – all buildings and the rest of the elements – so the next step was to find some good references. The search for references was an important part of the work; it was very useful for the modeling and texturing of the elements of the scene. For this image I searched for references on the internet, as well as using my small photographic library of photographic references of buildings in Madrid (**Fig.01a – c**).

Fig.01a

Fig.01b

© DE ANGELIS FABIO

Fig.01c

MODELING

Perhaps this is one of the scenes on which I have dedicated more time to the modeling; it's not a scene with complicated modeling, but it does contain many numbers of elements. The modeling work was divided into three parts: the modeling of the church, other buildings in the scene, and the rest of the elements that comprise the scene.

All modeling work was done in 3d Studio Max. I used the Edit Poly function to create the models; I always begin with standard primitive objects – a plane, a box, a cylinder or a sphere. I used splines to generate the basic forms to begin with. I usually convert these first forms to an editable poly or editable spline; with these tools you can generate

Fig.02a

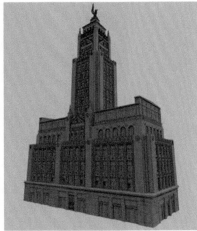

Fig.02b

Fig.02c

Fig.02d

modifications in parts of the geometry such as Extrude, Bevel, Chamfer or Cut. You can even use modifiers to deform or change the geometry, for example Noise, Displace, Push, Relax, Free Form Deformation, Bend and Taper. 3d Studio Max contains a great variety of modifiers that facilitate the work of the modeler.

I started by modeling the church (**Fig.02a**). For me, this was the most important object in the scene – it's not a complicated model, but does contain lots of elements and details that I wanted to show in the final scene. The first job was to create the facade and divisions to add the doors and windows. The next task was to create the different elements of the church – doors, arcs, cornice and the rest of the ornaments. The last work on this model was creating the roof and the vault.

Following my three-part process, I then modeled the rest of the buildings (**Fig.02b – c**). I gave all buildings in the scene a high level of detail. The modeling process is always the same for me: make the facade and generate divisions and the rest of the elements. In all processes I

Fig.04a

Fig.03

use references to create the most accurate and realistic models. The final stage of the modeling was to create the different elements of the street – traffic lights, streetlights, trash containers, light box, traffic signals, trees and so on (**Fig.02d**).

After modeling all objects, I composed the scene, which I find to be the most satisfying part of the process. The final scene was based on the real life references, and I was very pleased with the great final result, even without textures and lighting (**Fig.03**).

TEXTURING & SHADING

For the texturing process I created specific textures for lots of the objects (**Fig.04a – c**), and I also created some generic textures (**Fig.04d**). All textures for the scene were created in Photoshop. I used multiple references from my library of textures (dirt textures, base textures of brick, metal, wood, cement). For the rest of the textures in the scene I used references and photographs from cgtextures.com, which is a great source for texturing material.

For the materials in the scene, I used standard materials in Max – all used a Diffuse Map, Specular Map and in some cases I also used a Normal Map; the objects with a Reflection Map used Raytrace. This was a base shader for all geometry in the scene.

LIGHTING & RENDERING

For the lighting, I used one direct light with area shadows to simulate the light of the moon. I generated a dome light (in this case I used 45 spotlights incorporating a shadow map to create a hemisphere) to simulate a skylight; the

Fig.04b

Fig.04c

Fig.04d

result was very similar and the render time was fairly quick. Also in the scene I used Omni lights with shadow maps for the streetlights, and Omni lights to simulate light points in some areas of the scene (**Fig.05**).

For rendering, I used the Default Scanline Renderer of Max; I used the Catmull-Rom filter and activated Enable Global SuperSampler; the rest of parameters were left at default. The final image was calculated in one pass; the result of the render was very good and the first appearance of the image was really positive.

POST-PRODUCTION

For post-production I used only Combustion, and I made some adjustments to the final image. I used the Discreet

Fig.05

Color Corrector filter to adjust the saturation, contrast, and levels, and I also used the Balance, Brightness/Contrast and Color Shift filters to adjust the image color and brightness. Finally, as a last touch, I used the Glow filter to adjust the luminance of the image (**Fig.06**).

Fig.06

Conclusion

I've always liked modeling environments. When I look back to my first scenes I can see the evolution in my work – the models, textures and general quality. With each new work I create I can see the improvement over the previous project. I am very satisfied with the final result of this image and I am pleased to have been able to share the making of the image with you in this book. I hope you have enjoyed my small contribution.

Artist Portfolio

WALKWAY
BY GERHARD MOZSI

SOFTWARE USED: Photoshop CS3

THE START

The steps detailed here will explain the process of how I took an initial concept, based on a loose brief provided by *ImagineFX* magazine for their "Workshops", through to the final image that you see. For this piece, I was inspired by the mood of the film *Blade Runner* – a key starting point for any project is to get inspired and excited by the brief and your subject matter. I believe this is crucial actually, as it's this excitement that will motivate and push you through the darkest times of the project, when perhaps your image isn't quite working. After watching the *Blade Runner* movie and checking out some other artwork and photograph reference books for inspiration, I was ready to get started.

I had an image of a terminal or station in mind; a structure with an exposed roof revealing a tired, run-down city. I was thinking of a dark and moody setting, but with a sense of something grand, and so with the concept in mind I opened up Photoshop and created a new file. My approach for this image was to start by establishing a grid, using the Line tool, to create the perspective (**Fig.01**). Working with basic shapes first and foremost, I aimed to get them all down right at this stage, as doing so generally makes the detail easier to fill in. Getting them wrong will lead to a much harder job (as I actually discovered). So with the composition sorted, I added and

Fig.01

Fig.02

refined more detailed shapes, keeping the palette simple to avoid any confusion and to allow me to focus on my values.

At this stage I was feeling happy to start refining the image, which I generally do in passes, starting by ensuring my values were sitting right and then developing the palette. This whole process is a layered approach; everything sits in its own layer, which in turn sits in its own group. This becomes of benefit if and when you have to make changes – it makes it all quite easy (on the downside, however, your file size does get quite large when working this way). With this process, it's very important to name your groups and layers, as it can get very confusing very quickly (**Fig.02**).

Fig.03a

Things were going well here so I completed the day's session, went home and slept, thinking I'd resolved the composition's core elements. However, when I returned to the image the following day, I realized it wasn't working. To rescue the image I tried adding more color, more detail … but it still looked wrong. I realized that a complete compositional restructure was necessary, but I wanted to try a few tricks first to try and salvage the piece. So I added some photographic textures, some more dramatic lighting, more detail … to no avail. This was one of those dark moments I mentioned earlier: the picture just wasn't working (**Fig.03a – b**). I left the computer and forgot about it for a short while. Even when working on a deadline, a break for around five or ten minutes can really help to free the mind of any preconceived ideas about the image.

I returned to work on the image with a serious caffeine rush, accepting that I was going to have to change the composition. As it turned out, it wasn't too much hassle after all, and once the change had been made I felt invigorated and ready to get back to work. The solution was to simplify the composition; changing it to a big cross, adding a foreground element, but keeping the basic lighting and color scheme. I also got rid of my photographic textures, which added greater depth and drama to the image. I was happy that the revised image was now looking much better than before the compositional changes (**Fig.04**).

Fig.03b

Having elements play off one another is called a "counterpoint", which is crucial for adding drama and atmosphere to images. Playing with offsetting the horizontal against the vertical, cool colors with warm colors, saturated colors with unsaturated colors, soft edges with hard edges, and so on, I was able to bring interest to the image through the elements. It's all about contrast!

At this stage I could see how the image was going to develop, so I continued building up the detail, experimenting with more dramatic lighting and color (**Fig.05**). I find the easiest way to do this is to create a Soft Light layer and paint in the light and color, not

Fig.04

being shy and really pushing it! I generally aim to ruin the image with harsh color and light, and then work my way back by lowering the opacity – you can explore many options this way!

When detailing images, I generally use photos. There are no hard or fast rules for using photos in images, except that they are best used with subtlety. When used overtly, they can look really horrible! I've found the best layer modes to use when manipulating photos are Screen, Multiply, Soft Light and Overlay, all of which should be combined with a lower layer opacity for subtlety. Use Layer Masks rather than erasing – it can be a real annoyance having to drag the photo back into your file! I would also advise that texture strength is best controlled through the layer's opacity, as this gives you more control when it comes to tweaking later on.

When you take photos into your images, you need to paint them in so they sit well, color picking and painting over them to integrate them with the rest of your image, blending edges and tweaking along the way. The best way to check for any "matte lines" in your image is to create a Levels Adjustment layer and lighten the whole image – any odd matte lines should become obvious as you do this.

I find that when I think I'm coming close to finishing an image, I suddenly discover that I'm only half way there, and with this image it was no different. Painting the detail takes time; it requires patience and a passion for doing it (I personally enjoy listening to music when I'm painting in the details of an image). With the palette and lighting established, it was relatively straightforward to paint detail

Fig.05

Fig.06a

into the image, color picking from the painting. I chose to work around the image evenly, gradually and consistently building up detail (**Fig.06a – b**).

THE END

To achieve more intense contrast in the image, I held off on adding the highlights for as long as possible and darkened my shadows instead. This method worked well here because of all the bright neon signs. My final pass

Fig.06b

SCENES

was done with Adjustment Layers, creating a set with Color Balance, Levels and Photo Filter, experimenting with them and pushing them to their limits. The idea was simply to play with the Adjustment Layers until I achieved the level of drama and intensity I was seeking (**Fig.07**). This technique is particularly helpful if you've used lots of photos, as it helps to unify the image (the Photo Filter Adjustment Layer is good for this).

The image was set aside overnight and I went over it again the next day. A fresh set of eyes can really help you to reevaluate your image. Finally, show your work to as many people as you can – their opinions will be helpful!

Fig.07

ARTIST PORTFOLIO

STORY OF TIME 1981
BY HAO AI QIANG

SOFTWARE USED: 3d Studio Max, BodyPaint, V-Ray and Photoshop

INTRODUCTION

Everyone will remember a moment that has been lost in time to some extent or another; something which accompanied our life before perhaps being thrown away … I don't think this is their intended fate. I miss those objects that have been abandoned and so with this piece I wanted to think more about things that we discard from our lives, such as objects and memories, and as a result it became the driving motivation behind this artwork.

Fig.01

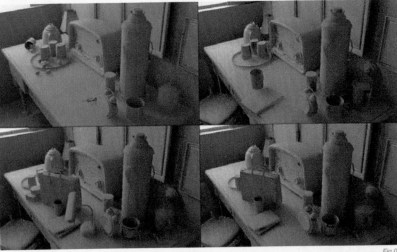

Fig.02

Fig.03

At the beginning, I drew a concept sketch and added some very simple light and shade to define the direction I wanted to take in 3D (**Fig.01**). All objects in the scene have been a part of my life at some point, but many of the details I can no longer remember clearly. As reference material I could only find pictures on the internet alongside material at flea markets – luckily I was able to collect all the required elements for this project for the objects I wanted to include.

MODELING

In 3d Studio Max I used basic geometry to build the initial layout of the scene. In order to grasp the overall ambience better, I set up simple lighting when there were only basic models in the scene (**Fig.02**). When I started adding the complete models to the scene, I rendered lots of drafts (**Fig.03**). This made it more targeted when adjusting the shapes and details of the model and layout (**Fig.04**).

TEXTURES & SHADERS

With this project, most of the textures were taken from the Total Textures collections; only a small part of the material was made by myself. The Total Textures are very high quality; nevertheless, I did have to adjust the color and brightness and paint some details using a special brush in Photoshop, or mix them with other textures using different blending modes (**Fig.05**).

Many of the textures needed to consider the model of the structure, so I did some texture painting in BodyPaint as

Fig.04

this was extremely necessary for certain objects in the project. BodyPaint can be painted in to a large extent to reduce UV seams (**Fig.06**).

Because I was rendering using V-Ray, I used a VRay Shader for speed and stability (**Fig.07**). Many of the objects needed to be aged, so I used a dirt map to control the reflection intensity to achieve the effects of aging on the reflected material, giving it a more worn and dusty feel (**Fig.08a – b**). The table top needed to appear to be greasy looking, so I used the interpolation mode glossy reflection of the VRay Shader, because this method of computing is the correct way to achieve this effect (**Fig.09**).

LIGHTING

In the final stage of the production, lighting the scene, the earlier preview of the lighting setup needed some adjustments, because the scene was to be illuminated by natural light. To achieve this, I used two area lights and a sphere light was used for the main light to simulate scattered sunlight (**Fig.10**), and a plane light was used

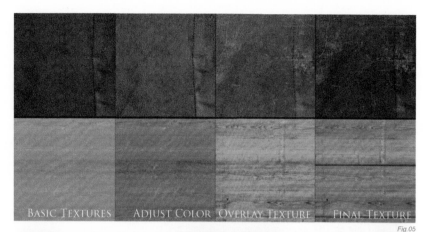

Fig.05

BASIC TEXTURES · ADJUST COLOR · OVERLAY TEXTURE · FINAL TEXTURE

Fig.06

Fig.07

REFLECTION CONTROL AND DIRT MASK

Fig.08a

REFLECTION CONTROL AND DIRT MASK

Fig.08b

Fig.09

to simulate sky light from the windows (**Fig.11**). The scene describes early morning, so the lighting tint leans towards a cooler color with an intensity that is not too high.

The size of the area lights had to be set very carefully because it affects the shape of the shadows, as well as the quality and render speed. With the settings complete, I rendered a lower Global Illumination (GI) map to check the color tones. From here I could then render some of the different tones and choose the best one (**Fig.12**).

RENDERING

In the V-Ray indirect illumination roll-out menu, I first of all set the primary bounces to Irradiance map and secondary bounces were assigned the Light Cache GI engine (**Fig.13**). In the V-Ray color mapping roll-out menu, I changed the Linear multiply type to Exponential (**Fig.14**). Using this color mapping mode keeps the image not too bright and not too dark. In addition, it also accelerates the speed of the GI calculation.

For the image sample setup I used the adaptive QMC mode. For the perfect image quality I set the minimum/maximum rate as 1/16, and set the color threshold to 0.00. Using these settings can decrease the noise in area shadows, glossy reflections and GI.

In the render element roll-out menu I added ZDepth and Render ID; these were then two automatically generated image files to be used for the final composition (**Fig.15**).

COMPOSITING

After rendering, the final image needed a lot of adjustments in the post–production software (Photoshop), such as the effect of depth of field (DOF). The direct

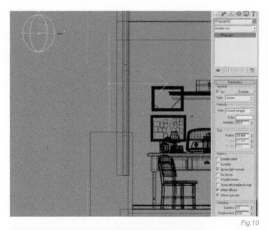

Fig.10

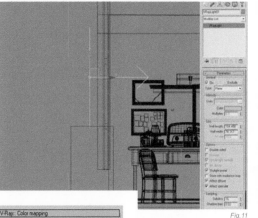

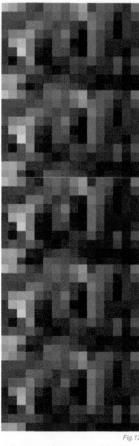

Fig.11   Fig.12

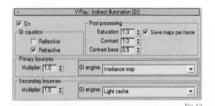

Fig.13   Fig.14

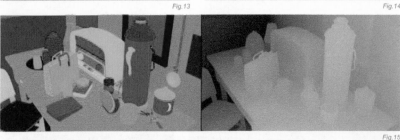

Fig.15

rendering was very slow, but the most important thing to remember is that a perfect effect from a final render is very difficult. Repeatedly making amendments to achieve the perfect final render will require an unacceptable amount of time.

When I adjust the contrast and color of my images I try to use adjustment layers. Through layer masks you can control and adjust the intensity of the variation; local parts can also be adjusted by editing a selection from the rendered file. In addition to all this, the final product output will reduce the loss of quality to a minimum (**Fig.16**).

CONCLUSION

Because of the added depth of field, the final image lost some of the original detail, but the main part of the image in turn became more prominent. Light from outdoors was also appropriate in order to strengthen and add a halo effect and glow together with other optical effects.

Whether the image would be close to a real photograph was not the only or main purpose of this project; what was important was that the image truly reflected the story behind the scene and conveyed the emotional aspect of the work. If we can perfect this, we will undoubtedly create outstanding works!

ORIGINAL RENDER   DOF EFFECT

ADJUST EXPOSURE   ADJUST COLOR

Fig.16

BUGGY SERIES
BY MAREK DENKO

SOFTWARE USED: 3d Studio Max, V-Ray and Photoshop

INTRODUCTION

The image I'm going to discuss here is part of my 2008 personal project, which I refer to as the *Buggy Series*, in which I created a big, rusty fallout style buggy and rendered it in several different environments. For the purposes of this book I'm going to be referring to the desert environment, and in the following article I'll describe my procedures and processes of creation for this particular scene.

Fig.01

© MAREK DENKO

It all started in the beginning of 2008 at a time when I had a bit of freedom from my professional work, and I already had this idea in mind. I admit that the concept is not really anything new or revolutionary, but the idea behind it was that it would be a gift for my son, Adam, who was

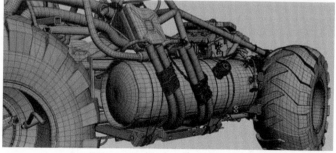

Fig.03

Fig.02

just nine months old when I finished this project. I hope that when he's older it will be printed for his bedroom wall. I'd also been watching the *Mad Max* trilogy and had fallen in love with the mood of post apocalyptic movies such as these, and I decided to create my own fallout machine with a similar feeling/mood in the final illustrations.

Over the following pages I'd like to share a few words about this project, step by step, starting from the searching of references through the modeling, texturing, shading, lighting and rendering to the final post-production.

CONCEPT & REFERENCES

There was no sketch or one main reference used for the buggy; the whole design was created on the fly with lots of playing around and moving parts here and there. I did spend several hours, however, searching through the internet and my photographic library to find nice pictures of elements which would be suitable for this project; I searched for old engines, rusty wheels, jet engines and all those kinds of interesting things. I always find references to be an essential part of my work. After a couple of years creating CG images you have a lot of things already in your mind's eye, but sometimes when you look at your references you can find a lot of interesting things and details which are very hard to realize if you don't see them directly. They are very helpful for the most part in the process of modeling, texturing and shading.

MODELING

All modeling work was done in 3d Studio Max. For the modeling of objects like the wheels, engine and basically all metal objects, I used Editable Poly, which is one of the most commonly used modeling techniques in the industry. Everyone who wants to start with computer graphics should know this modeling technique very well; it is one of the most popular methods of modeling. For me, modeling is just a routine part of the work,

Fig.04

but I still like to do it very much. When I'm modeling, in most cases I start from primitive objects, like a plane, box, cylinder, sphere or even shapes like a line, circle or rectangle, and after a few deformations I usually convert them to an Editable Poly or Editable Spline. Then it is only about selections, extruding, beveling, chamfering, cutting – and all those modeling tools which are available in your 3D package (which in this case is 3d Studio Max). Very often I use several types of modifiers to deform or change the geometry; for example, Symmetry, Bend, Twist, Taper, Free Form Deformer, Noise, Displace, Turbosmooth, Wave, Ripple, Path Follow, etc. If you are a beginner in 3D modeling you should read the manual of your 3D package and try to find out how it works. You can trust me that modeling static objects is one of the easier parts of 3D. If you want to be a fast, good and precise modeler you need to know your modeling tools as well as possible. So take the time to read about them and try them out.

Fig.05

Fig.06

All heavy, rusty metal objects were modeled with the Editable Poly technique, as mentioned (**Fig.01 – 04**). For the grass in the scene, I modeled a few types of strands with very few polygons only, and then scattered them with the script called Advanced Painter by Herman Saksono, upgraded by my friend Federico Ghirardini (script is free and you can find it on scriptspot.com). I created several different grass groups and then randomly placed them in the scene. I was quite satisfied with that, but it still missed some variation and irregularity. For the stones, I created several levels of detail. I then used Particle Flow to scatter a few types of stone on the base geometry. High resolution stones were used for the foreground, medium for the more distant stones, and low polygonal ones for the background (**Fig.05 – 06**).

Fig.07

TEXTURING & SHADING

For texturing I use Photoshop. When it comes to texturing I mostly use textures from photographs, and sometimes, if necessary, I paint some details by hand (**Fig.07 – 11**). There are some very nice texture sites on the internet, such as Environment-Textures. com and cgtextures.com. I also used lots of dirt textures from 3DTotal's Total Textures

Fig.09

Fig.08

Fig.10

Fig.11

collections; I actually consider the dirt collection from 3DTotal to be one of the best texture collections available.

Since I was going to use V-Ray to render this image, I used VRayMtl as a base shader for all the geometry (**Fig.12**). Very often I use a low intensity of Fresnel glossy reflections. In general raytraced reflections increase render times, but they also help to achieve a more natural and believable looking image.

Fig.12

Fig.13

LIGHTING & RENDERING

For rendering I used V-Ray from Chaos Group, which is a very good renderer used mainly in architectural visualization but is also frequently used for movies and commercials. Basically, there are two lights in the scene – one is a directional light (key light) simulating the sun with a yellowish color and hard shadows, since the sun is very high in the desert during the day, and the second light (fill light) is a sky dome with a VRay sky map. I used also Global Illumination bounces to produce more realistic results.

POST-PRODUCTION

For post–production I usually use Photoshop or Fusion. This time, since it was a pretty high resolution image (6000 pixels wide) and Photoshop

is much faster using color correction, I decided to go with it. The sky in the background was hand painted. I did a lot of color correction to the render and I also painted over a few details and covered a few spots I didn't like (**Fig.13 – 14**). Everything was done in 16-bit/channel color depth to protect the color information as much as possible.

CONCLUSION

So that's it! It was not really difficult to make this image. The hardest part was to find the time and will to proceed and finish it. I believe that if you've read all of this then you should understand some of my techniques and how I work. I'm certainly not saying that my way is the only way and the right way, but hopefully this insight can be of some use to your own projects.

Fig.14

Gaz M20 Pobeda aka Warszawa

By Piotr Luziński

Software Used: 3d Studio Max, V-Ray and Photoshop

Introduction

The story behind the development of my series of renders based on the Pobeda car (manufactured in Poland under the name Warszawa) is nothing uncommon – it happened purely by accident and quite spontaneously. It started when I was asked to model a car for my friend, which I never would have thought of doing myself previously. I'm not too keen on old automobiles, so I initially had no desire to push the car designs any further. However, after completing the model I suddenly had a brainstorm and thought it would be a good idea to refresh my portfolio. I then came across the superb HDRI maps and backgrounds on 3SIX0.net (**Fig.01**) which offered me a perfect opportunity to render my model in an outdoor environment.

I was pretty sure at the time that I was going to take the Nissan GTR that I had completed previously into the

Fig.01

Photograph by Piotr Luzinski

Fig.02a

Photograph by Piotr Luzinski

Fig.02c

Photograph by Piotr Luzinski

Fig.02b

3SIX0 environment, but my friend convinced me that I should do something more unusual and rarely seen. And it was then that the idea of modeling the Pobeda was born, and I have to admit that the idea has since proven to be bang on!

Modeling

Good reference images are the key to a successful model, and at the time I was lucky enough to find blueprints of the car, and also took some photographs of the car taped up geometrically (**Fig.02a – c**). These photos and blueprints, together with the "camera match" in 3d Studio Max, allowed me to reproduce a model of the original car with extreme precision.

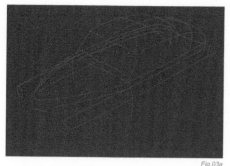

Fig.03a

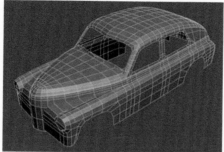

Fig.03b

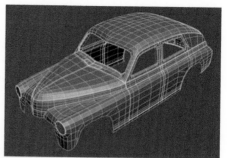

Fig.03c

As usual, I started by drawing NURBS curves through the major lines and cuts of the chassis, in order to achieve a kind of 3D grid. This grid made it possible for me to carry out slight corrections immediately by making modifications on only several points of the curves, instead of moving a large number of vertices (which can often lead to the loss of smoothness). But first and foremost, it served as a guideline for the polygonal wireframe and guaranteed perfect roundness.

The next step was to form the major surfaces of the model, which in my case slightly resembles modeling in CAD software because the surfaces are not mutually joined immediately but instead interpenetrate each other. The point here was that I was aiming to weld points only when I was absolutely sure that all mutually adjacent surfaces were as smooth as possible (**Fig.03a – d**). From time to time I also found it good to take a look at whether the model results matched the photos, and in such a case the "camera match" tool was irreplaceable (**Fig.04**).

Upon completion of the main body I then got down to the model details. The rule is very simple: the more detail, the better, particularly if enlarged views or close-ups of the model are anticipated (**Fig.05**). When I was sure that all of the modeling work was considered satisfactory and complete, it was time to start the next stage of work.

Materials & Texturing

My projects usually need only a few textures, due to the fact that I currently mainly deal with the modeling of high-poly automobiles and so the texturing ends up as

Fig.03d

PHOTOGRAPH BY PIOTR LUZINSKI

Fig.04

simply a bump for the lamps, brake disks, and so on. But with this image I wanted to take a step beyond the usual, in order to achieve the most realistic image possible. As an example, the tree for the tire materials has been detailed in **Fig.06**.

One of the most important roles was assigned to the displacement technique that was applied to the headlights, indicators, lateral surfaces of the tires, and the logos on the bonnet. Although there are many people who would oppose this method and who would prefer to model all the components, I personally believe that displacement has some

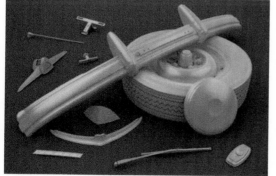

Fig.05

indisputable advantages. First and foremost, it never results in the increase of triangles in the scene, which, in the case of modeling, may result in a dramatic slowdown of viewport rotation. In addition, it also keeps the wireframe undistorted and never forces you to increase its density before adding detail, which facilitates further editing of the surfaces, if necessary.

The second thing that played an important role was the selection of textures for dirty areas, mainly on the wheels and nearby. For this project, in every case these textures were mixtures of several layers, but rather than joining them together in Photoshop I did it all in the Material Editor with the use of masks, where procedural maps, such as cellular, splat or stucco, were redirected. This allowed me to monitor and make corrections to all the settings on a regular basis, in order to search for the best effect.

The next indispensable component was VRay Dirt, which was applied virtually everywhere, from the car paint to single nuts. Thanks to this tool, all grooves and joins became more distinct, which allowed me to achieve more detail in the rendered images (**Fig.07a – b**).

I also couldn't ignore the texturing of the car's interior (**Fig.08**). Interiors are hardly visible, but they do play an important role and help to achieve the most realistic reproduction of the whole view as possible. To design

Fig.06

Fig.07a

Fig.07b

Fig.08

Fig.09a

Fig.09b

Fig.09c

these textures I used various photographs, but in most cases they had to be adjusted in Photoshop to alter the existing perspective or remove any undesired reflections.

At this stage, all my preparations were complete and it was time to get down to testing everything in the scene (**Fig.09a – c**).

LIGHTING & RENDERING
The starting point is always the same: materials are at hand, all the settings are set, so I simply click the magic

button "Render" … and it's then that I can see just how much work is to be done! This is how one of my first renders looked when I was testing the car paint material and lighting (**Fig.10a**). I was pretty disheartened, but I quickly launched Photoshop and after some quick fun with various sliders I got something like this (**Fig.10b**). So I had myself a reference point and knew what kind of effect I was aiming for directly in 3d Studio Max, and I managed to reach the desired objective after a period of time (**Fig.10c**). With the initial base done I then started to add subsequent materials to improve (or perhaps worsen) the already prepared models (**Fig.10d**).

As you can see, there was still a long way to go at this stage until the final version of the image, especially because I wanted do everything nearly perfect in all areas, so I continued with my experiments on each component, one after another. You can see how

Fig.10a

Fig.11a

Fig.10b

Fig.11b

Fig.11c

Fig.10c

Fig.10d

Fig.11d

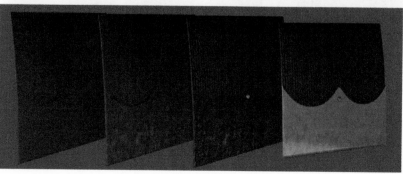

Fig.12

subsequent metamorphoses of the vehicle looked, for example in the case of the headlights (**Fig.11a – d**), wheels (**Fig.12**) or even mud flaps (**Fig.13**).
This was just a small fragment of a long series of trial renders that I had to produce in order to achieve the effects that can be seen in the following close-ups (**Fig.14a – e**).

Following all the experiments, all that was left to do was to find the final and interesting take, and I also had some

Fig.13

fun playing with various colors for the paintwork (**Fig.15**). It was really hard choosing a single version, so I made a few different final images, some of which can be seen in the Artist Portfolio section.

So much hassle went into achieving the best possible effects directly from 3d Studio Max, that the only post-production needing to be done at the end was cropping the images, some subtle color correction, adding some noise and vignette ... and that was it!

Fig.14a

Fig.14b

Fig.14c

Fig.14d

Fig.14e

CONCLUSION

The entire project was a great leap forward for me, as I've always found rendering a troublesome operation. It was the first time I'd driven a model from an indoor studio setup into the open air, so I found myself in a completely new environment. In addition to this, I also learned some of the rules of composition, which was enforced due to the fact that the background was taken from real photos and the entire image had to be properly balanced. I also spent a lot of time-consuming work with the materials – much more time than ever before.

All in all, it was the most demanding project I have ever done, but it was also the one that has given me the most satisfaction and joy after the final effect was reached. For a graphic designer there is no better prize than to read appreciating opinions on the completed job, and the fact that my work is in this book is clear evidence that it was worth trying hard. Thank you for staying with me to the end of this article; I hope that it has been as interesting for you to read it as it was for me to write.

ARTIST PORTFOLIO

1944
BY SAREL THERON

SOFTWARE USED: Photoshop and LightWave 3D

INTRODUCTION

I have always been intrigued by those old World War II aviation oil paintings that one occasionally comes across in history books. The mood and atmosphere are often almost tangible, together with those wintry skies and muted palettes – so evocative of that darkest hour in human history. My aim was to capture the feeling of those old paintings while depicting the very intense fighting over the Crimean peninsula in 1944 as the Axis forces started making their withdrawal from the Caucasus. I think one of the things that make this image unique is the variety of elements that went into its creation. It consists of a combination of practical models, computer 3D models, photographs and digital painting.

CONCEPT

As per my usual procedure, I started off with a color concept sketch using Photoshop (**Fig.01**). This not only helps me work out the composition, color palette and lighting, but also establishes the overall mood of the painting. Rather than blithely following the ubiquitous rule of thirds with regards to composition, I opted instead for an iconic layout, positioning the warplanes in the middle of the canvas. I'm always conscious of how color and

Fig.01

light can be used to define the focal point in a painting, and have used these elements to good effect in laying the focus primarily on the warplanes.

Another important consideration for me was in creating a sufficient amount of atmospheric perspective to help give a sense of depth to the painting. Atmospheric perspective defines our perception of objects as they recede into the distance. The further away an object gets, the lighter the tone becomes, whilst colors tend to cool and contrasts lessen. Additionally, the correct application of linear perspective was critical in establishing a convincing aerial viewpoint. Linear perspective is a system for drawing objects that uses lines and vanishing points to determine how much an object's apparent size changes with space.

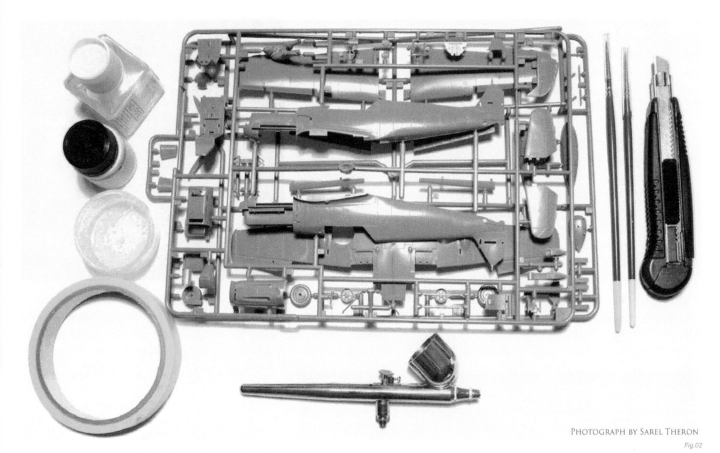

Fig.02

Color can also be very effective in creating mood, and so I opted for a gray, muted – almost monochromatic – palette that gives the painting a feeling of age, reminiscent of the color photographs of that era.

MODELING

A 1/48th scale warplane (**Fig.02**) was constructed from an off-the-shelf plastic kit. One could of course have created a CG 3D model instead, but building an actual physical model is so much more fun! It also gave me the opportunity to dust off my faithful old airbrush (which has been in retirement since the turn of the millennium) and put it to good use in painting and weathering the model. Once the aircraft model was complete, I took numerous

Fig.03

photographs of it from various angles against a chroma key backdrop (**Fig.03**).

The naval base and industrial area were created in LightWave 3D (**Fig.04**). These were built using primitives in LightWave's Modeler with a little definition added using the Polygon Pen tool. Aerial photographs of the 1943 Ploesti Refinery raid over Romania were referenced in order to bring a degree of authenticity to the industrial-style architecture.

Being an unabashed detail junkie, I inevitably had to create some smaller 3D models, such as AA artillery

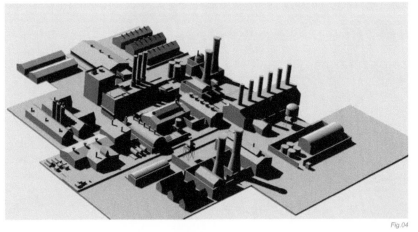

Fig.04

guns, tanks, cranes and ships in an effort to add some further interest to the landscape (**Fig.05**). Once all the modeling was complete, the various elements were brought together in Layout and properly positioned, scaled and lit. The shaded geometry was then rendered out at about 4k, after having established the correct perspective and lighting by referencing my concept sketch. I did not apply any textures to the models as this, and all the other detail, was to be painted in Photoshop later.

COMPOSITING & PAINTING

Opening my concept sketch in Photoshop again, I started refining the sky by referencing my personal library of cloud photographs (**Fig.06**). The technique I use for creating skies in all of my paintings is to cut out any interesting cloud formations, pasting them over each other and blending everything together with a lot of paint on top. This matte painting technique often allows for the creation of some very dramatic cloudscapes, the likes of which rarely occur in nature. Interestingly, the black oily smoke was also created with photographs of clouds.

Next, I started laying down the 3D renderings of the buildings over the sketch (**Fig.07**). The textures were then painted over the shaded geometry using standard brushes with liberal daubs from the Clone Stamp tool. There was a lot of nitty-gritty one pixel detailing involved here, and it was probably one of the most time-consuming parts of the painting.

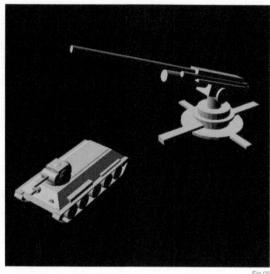

Fig.05

The same scale model was referenced for the various aircraft. In order to create some disparity between the individual aircraft, photographs taken from slightly different angles were used. Additionally the aircraft numbers and camouflage patterns were also changed in Photoshop (**Fig.08**). The spinning propellers were painted in by hand with a little Radial Blur applied via the Filters menu. Lastly, I made heavy use of the Dodge tool to simulate the effect of sunlight reflecting off the aircrafts' aluminum skin and glass canopies.

CONCLUSION

If I had more time (and an infinite amount of patience), I would probably have covered the entire landmass with 3D buildings, as per my original concept sketch. Also, in order to add some extra ambience I could have rendered a few flak bursts or streams of tracer fire, although one has to be careful not to overdo these kinds of visual effects. All in all, I'm quite pleased with the final result as is, and hopefully I've managed to capture the feel of those old WWII oil paintings.

© SAREL THERON

Fig.06

Fig.07

Fig.08

THE PURSUIT
BY THIBAUT MILVILLE

SOFTWARE USED: 3d Studio Max, V-Ray and Photoshop

INTRODUCTION

This image is the first of a series devoted to the 1970s American muscle cars. For this illustration, I wanted to pay tribute to all those old road chase movies, so I began by collecting references from inspirational films using the Internet Movie Cars Database (imcdb.org). This website is a great source of references; you simply choose the car model you're interested in modeling and the search engine gives you a list of films in which the car has been credited. Once I'd found some inspirational material for the scene, I then searched for a background that would fit in with the mood of the scene – a road in the middle of nowhere.

The choice of cars for this illustration was easy. My aim was to represent a powerful muscle car, famous in the movies of the 1970s, with a contemporary police car. The cop car had to be a threat to the muscle car, and I

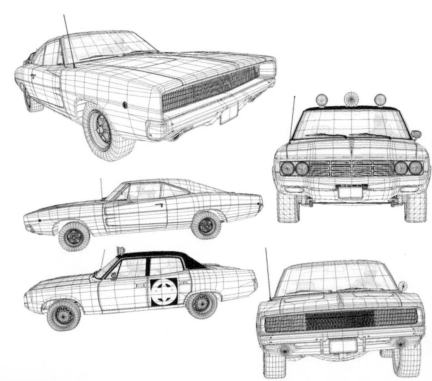

Fig.01

Fig.02

thought that bright headlights would give it a predator-type look. I also wanted the image to evoke the sensation of great speed, and to show that the pursuit had reached its apex.

MODELING

The modeling was based on blueprints available for both models. I won't explain how to model a car with blueprints; high quality tutorials already exist on this and you can find lots of good quality blueprints on the internet. There are great websites that provide free downloads, such as the-blueprints.com, smcars.net or suurland.com.

The first car was modeled with great precision because I knew I'd like to re-use it for other illustration projects (because I'm really fond of this particular car model, I

Fig.03

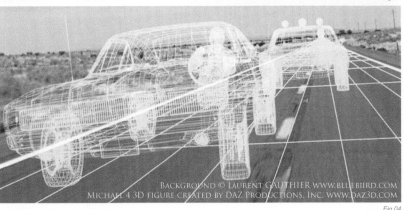

BACKGROUND © LAURENT GAUTHIER WWW.BLUEBIIRD.COM
MICHAEL 4 3D FIGURE CREATED BY DAZ PRODUCTIONS, INC. WWW.DAZ3D.COM

Fig.04

plan to render some close-up shots and integrate them into a vintage advert recreation soon). However, the second car was less detailed because it was always going to be partly hidden by the headlight effect, and I wasn't planning on reusing the model again. **Fig.01** shows the wireframes of the models.

Because the characters were not main elements in the illustration I chose not to waste any time modeling them and instead imported DAZ 3D free models, textured and rigged in 3d Studio Max.

SHADING & TEXTURING

I created very simple materials that looked as realistic as I could get them (car-paint, chrome, glass, rubber and so on) and then created a very rough and matte dust material. Both vehicles were shaded with a clean material and then covered with a layer of dust; the amount of dust was controlled by a grayscale mask. Depending on the material, this mask was either painted in Photoshop or was a mix of a procedural smoke and a VRayDirt map. **Fig.02** illustrates the effect of the dirt map.

Tires were modeled simply; details were rendered with a displacement map. In order to save time during the rendering process, I built a "tire texture pack" so that I could apply the right texture for the right speed, and it was much faster than computing real motion blur. I also used a space deformation to simulate the weight of the cars and the flatness of the tires. You can see an extract of my texture pack and how it works whilst rendering in **Fig.03**.

COMPOSITION

The difficulty with this image was to make the viewer believe that the cars were really on the road. To manage this, I had to solve two problems: the perspective of the scene had to match the background, and the reflections had to show the environment around the cars.

© LAURENT GAUTHIER
(WWW.BLUEBIIRD.COM)

Fig.05a

Fig.06a

Fig.05b

Fig.06b

Fig.05c

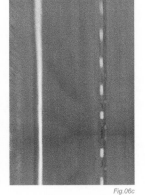

Fig.06c

The scene was very simple: a road, two cars and a desert environment. A directional light simulated the sun and the camera was manually positioned so that the wire road matched the background. The cars were then put in the right place to create a feeling of tension in the pursuit. In order to help me during the construction of the image, I animated the whole scene and chose the frame that gave me the right feeling. You can see the scene wireframe in **Fig.04**.

THE BACKGROUND

I chose a clean background which was too sharp and gave no impression of speed (**Fig.05a**), so I needed to add some motion blur to it. It had a small vanishing point, and a zoom blur could have made the sensation of speed. But this sort of blur effect was constant all over the picture and it didn't give the right feeling (**Fig.05b**). Only the elements close to the camera should be blurred; distanced elements had to remain sharp. So I built an infinite plane to model the ground. The background was baked on this plane thanks to the camera mapping. I then used a dolly camera that moved as the spectator, and I rendered the scene with motion blur (**Fig.05c**). That did the job!

TEXTURING THE ROAD

To make the texture of the road I used the same camera mapping as for the background (**Fig.06a**). A render to texture gave me a raw map (**Fig.06b**), and after a few edits I had a texture that perfectly fitted the environment (**Fig.06c**).

Fig.07

Fig.08

PAINTING THE ENVIRONMENT

To render believable reflections I needed an environmental texture which was compatible with the background. I put a camera at the center of my scene and rendered an equirectangular picture of the spherical environment. As a blueprint, this picture gave me the lines of the environment in order to paint my spherical map (**Fig.07**); it was not aesthetic, but very effective. I then added the sky and natural elements to reproduce

Fig.09

an environment that fitted with the background (**Fig.08**). (As long as you pay attention to the Creative Commons license, you can find free and high quality equirectangular images on flickr.com which could help you to create your own environments.) A test render with a chrome sphere at the center of the scene allowed me to validate the quality of the texture (**Fig.09**).

RENDERING & POST-PRODUCTION

The scene was illuminated by a directional light which simulated the sun, and a contrasted environment texture was used as a dome light. Specular effects were rendered partially and retouched in Photoshop, and the lens flare effects were created and tweaked in Photoshop. The image was then reconstructed from the different V-Ray passes (**Fig.10a – b**), and after a slight motion blur and color correction, the process was complete.

CONCLUSION

This image took a lot of my time to get it finished, but I learned so much more from the creative process than I could have expected, and I'm pleased to have been able to share my experience with you. I certainly hope you've enjoyed reading this.

Fig.10a

Fig.10b

ARTIST PORTFOLIO

© THIBAUT MILVILLE 2008

© THIBAUT MILVILLE 2008

© THIBAUT MILVILLE 2008

© THIBAUT MILVILLE 2009

ICE CITY
BY TITUS LUNTER

SOFTWARE USED: Photoshop CS3

IN THE BEGINNING...

For me, the motivation to make a piece is always easy to find, being curious by nature and a workaholic by choice. At the time when I made this piece I was so obsessed with my schoolwork that creativity was being forced out of me, which any artist will tell you is not the way it's supposed to work. So when I had the opportunity to step outside the box – if only a little – I grabbed the opportunity with both hands and created my *Ice City*.

NARRATIVE

One of the key things for me is having a story – no matter what shape or form, as long it's something quantifiable. So when I started on this piece based on a short story, tons of ideas were running through my head. It all started with an assignment to create a short story designed to place predesigned characters into a new environment; in this case a very unforgiving one. Starting off with the setting was, in this case, purely derived from the constraints given by the narrative that was written. In any case, I needed to make a matte painting – or two to be exact – in about eight hours, to give a proof of concept. I found an ideal backplate for my matte on Flickr, in the form of a photograph taken by the photographer, Egor Erchov (aka Kaldoon) (**Fig.01**). In approximately four hours I had created the *Ice City*.

APPROACH

When you're dealing with huge time issues, but you still want to deliver a good looking – or close enough to it – image, a certain amount of creative thinking is required. Not necessarily in the actual technical aspect, but more so in the way of dealing with the problem. The one thing

Fig.01

Fig.02

that I wanted to capture was the right atmosphere, without having to add a lot of custom detail that would take up a lot of time and effort. So the first thing I did was to analyze the topic: what it was that I needed to make and how I would achieve it as quickly as possible.

The story took place in a post apocalyptic world in which a new ice age was setting in. Between storms a team of people had to move camp, so an image was required showing the impact of an ice age on a metropolis. The key features for me to show were the cold and the color distortion. I broke the image down into several depths (**Fig.02**): the main detail depth, the color distortion depth (focusing heavily on atmospheric perspective), and the light in the background. After that I blocked in all the details roughly, and determined which buildings needed extra attention (**Fig.03**). The trick with digital painting is that you almost have too much luxury and freedom. When you're stressed for time, but have the tendency to

Fig.03

Fig.04

be really meticulous, the possibility to keep changing stuff will often cost the most time.

THE WALKTHROUGH

So with time being the prime factor, finding the focal points and adjusting the frame of the image was the hardest and most important part. The building cluster on the right of the image, of which the central point is the big black building, serves as the contra-weight of the light source above it. To ease the eye back into the rest of the image the detail was increased in the middle of the piece. On the opposite end, an eye catcher in the form of building lights serves as an alternate visual path (**Fig.04**).

One thing that is difficult to manage is the color balance of an image. In this case I used some pretty basic lighting techniques to blend the lighting used in the work in progress files to get everything to match up (**Fig.05**). Throughout the complete production stage I kept in mind the fact that the balancing in this image had to be just right, in order to achieve the strongest atmosphere and feel possible. Flipping the image was a regular

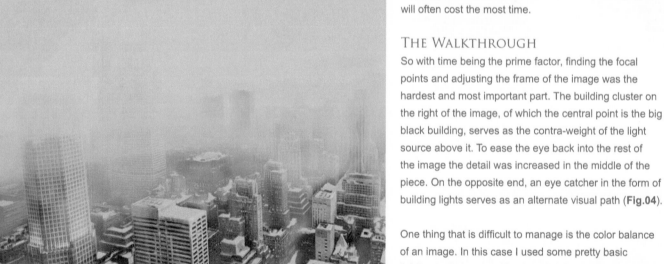

Fig.05

occurrence, which I did to check where my colors were pushing the image towards.

One of the final touches I gave the image was the snow (**Fig.06**). Again, the time issue forced me to use a technique that was cheesy, but did its job. By making a black and white layer, then applying the cloud filter, I was able to use the Texture > Texturizer option (**Fig.07**). By setting this to canvas it gave me the scattered feel I was looking for. The layer option was then set to Soft Light to hide the rough detail, leaving only the snow-like pattern. This layer was modified with the directional blur filter afterwards, instead of regular rotation, to take some of the extra "edge" off it.

Finally, the grain was applied to the entire image to mimic surface distortion. As snow can leave an irregular pattern when winds are blowing, having to paint all that detail in

Fig.06

would've been a nightmare! Carefully applied grain suggested the presence of surface distortion, and thus brought the image more "together".

CONCLUSION

All the decisions I made when I was making this were on the fly; everything was based on the plate itself. There are of course many things I would've done differently if there was enough time to create a more intricate composite of images, but since I had to do it with only this one image I was pretty much bound by its layout. This constraint, however, pushed me to find new limits and allowed me to achieve this work. All in all, I'm pleased with the result and the new tricks it has taught me.

Fig.07

ARTIST PORTFOLIO

PAWNSHOP
BY TOMÁŠ KRÁL

SOFTWARE USED: 3d Studio Max, finalRender and Photoshop

INTRODUCTION

Some time ago we – me and some friends – came up with an idea to make a game … we later named the project, "Ashfall". Purely for our own satisfaction, we started putting together various ideas, thoughts and, of course, numerous graphical concepts. Ashfall was always meant to be a 2.5D adventure game with a very strong story, where a fully 3D character moves freely on a pre-rendered back plate. My task on this project was to work on these pre-rendered environments. Here, I'll talk you through my process of creating one of these environments.

CONCEPT & REFERENCES

At the very beginning of any project I usually pick up lots of references; either I shoot them myself or search the internet on the likes of Google or Flickr. This part of the project is very important for my work as it helps tremendously later on when texturing, modeling details or creating materials and so on.

In the case of this project, we were overwhelmed with various ideas for what the visual style of our game should look like, so it was essential for us to write everything down on paper for later reference. Our team spent countless hours discussing and sketching so that we all settled on the general look and feel of the world our game was going to be set in (**Fig.01**).

Fig.01

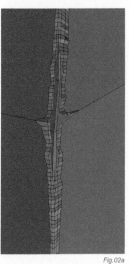

Fig.02a

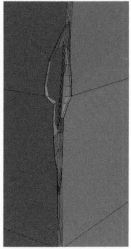

Fig.02b

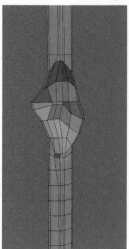

Fig.02c

MODELING & COMPOSITION

The modeling in this project wasn't too difficult; I started with very simple primitives, like boxes, planes and cylinders. Then the almost endless toying around with Editable Poly tools like extrude, bevel, cut, and plenty of chamfering, started. Since the output of this piece was supposed to be a still image, I didn't have to bother too much with stuff that was going to be outside of the rendered frame, which is why before any detailed modeling began I created a camera and set it up from where I wanted to see my scene. Using very simple geometry I made an approximate composition.

Every object that you create in 3D is geometrically perfect, which is not possible in reality, which is why it's always a good idea to break and distort your models a bit, to make them slightly imperfect. Using tools like cut, extrude or chamfer you can easily add various holes, scratches and beveled edges, and therefore break that 3D perfection (**Fig.02a – c**). And if your model has enough geometrical resolution, you can also add a few more irregularities to it using the noise modifier.

Fig.03a

Fig.03b

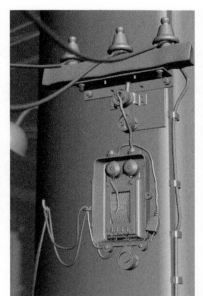

Fig.03c

Fig.03d

PROPS

The scene is filled with lots of small, seemingly non-essential props. These objects are also made using the same basic Editable Poly tools. Their function is to fill out the scene and thus make the final render a bit more interesting for the viewer. These props also have the advantage of being copied all over the place again and again, once you have them modeled (**Fig.03a – d**).

MAPPING

The worst and least fun part of a project, if you ask me, is the mapping. There are fantastic programs, such as UVLayout, that can help you a lot, but I've found that UVLayout is better suited to mapping organic or more complex models. This is why I use standard, simple UV mapping techniques much more often. Simple planar, cubic or cylindrical mapping with a tileable texture got the job done this time. For more complex objects, I used the unwrap tools.

To preview the UV distortion on my models, I didn't use the 3d Studio Max standard checker map but instead a special texture map created by Loocas Duber, with numbers and letters on it, which helped me a lot when looking at the mapped mesh and made it much more readable (**Fig.04**).

Fig.04

TEXTURES

For texture creation I use Photoshop. I like to think about my scenes as if they are a story. What happened there over the years, what kind of people lived there, what kind of an environment is the scene set in? The city in which our game story has been set is full of dark passages, old half-ruined buildings and all kinds of dirty corridors. I also like to take pictures of textures myself, but in this case the Total Textures DVDs from 3DTotal were a priceless asset in the image creation – especially Volume 5, which contains lots of dirt maps. By combining those dirt maps together in Photoshop I was able to get exactly the type of dirty surface textures I was seeking (**Fig.05a – c**).

Fig.05a

Fig.05b

Fig.05c

Lighting & Rendering

Since this is a nighttime scene, the main sources of light naturally come from the windows of the pawnshop and the lamp in the back street. To make the light coming from the window look a bit more interesting, I filled parts of the window space with torn-apart blinds. The scene was also lit with a bunch of additional lights, such as the orange light of the burning barrel of flames (**Fig.06**).

For the rendering I used a third party renderer called finalRender, for several reasons. First of all, I understand it quite well; secondly it was a fair trade between quality and render times. I like to use Global Illumination in conjunction with my manual lighting, and finalRender has, at least at present, the best and fastest GI on the market. Also, to gain a bit more flexibility in the post-production stage, I rendered along with the standard beauty pass, several other passes, such as specular, shadows, ID, ambient occlusion, ZDepth and so on (**Fig.07a – c**).

Post-Production

I heard somewhere that the pure render you get from your renderer is like a raw diamond, and this idea grew in my heart. I like to use all the available methods which can help me to achieve the best possible final artwork. As I mentioned earlier, my output was a still image, hence my choice of program for the final post-production was Photoshop (**Fig.08**). The main correction was the overall color of the scene. I made many color corrections so that the whole picture had a cold, turquoise tint which was supposed to feel a bit unsettling and dark. Contrary to this, I colored the window of the pawnshop with a rich orange to make this part of the image attract the viewers' attention the most, and also to create a feeling between the relatively safe place and the disturbing darkness. In the end I painted a few spider webs in certain places and added a light glow around the pawnshop window and lamp (**Fig.09a – d**).

Fig.06

AMBIENT OCCLUSION

Fig.07a

Z-DEPTH

Fig.07b

ID-PASS

Fig.07c

Fig.08

Fig.09a

Fig.09b

CONCLUSION

I learned a lot of new things in this project and without a doubt it was beautiful to watch a world we dreamed of unfold in our hands. Unfortunately, we never found an investor or a publisher, so this project will sadly end as an unfinished dream. But I'm happy at least to be sharing this article with you and to pay tribute to this unfinished game, on which we spent the greatest times. I'd also like to thank my friends Filip, Michal, Ondra and Honza, who all worked with me on this project.

Fig.09c

Fig.09d

ARTIST PORTFOLIO

COUCH BY THE WINDOW
BY VIKTOR FRETYÁN

SOFTWARE USED: 3d Studio Max and Photoshop

INTRODUCTION

I was browsing through one of my sister's interior design catalogues one day when I came across an advertisement for a company selling hard wood floors. There were a lot of things happening in the scene, such as pieces of the parquet flooring flying upwards in a pattern, as if they were dancing, and a girl on the couch listening to music. Since I'm involved in architectural visualization, all that really caught my attention in the image (and what would probably have been the last for anyone else) was the powerful composition of three elements: the camera view, window and the couch. I no longer have the advertisement as a reference, but I was surprised to find that my scene achieved an equally powerful composition, if not more powerful than the advert I once saw.

I study architecture at university and have been working in 3D for four years now, although I have known 3d Studio Max since version 2; I work for about 12 hours a day using Max and am always excited about the end of whichever project is current so I can concentrate on the next, as well as my own personal projects. The particular piece, *Couch by the Window*, is one of my personal works, and so far I would say it has become one of my favorites. The whole project took just one night to create

Fig.01a

from scratch. It's a very simple scene, but this simplicity is possibly the major part of its essence. I think the end result turned out to be really powerful.

MODELING & LIGHTING

I modeled everything from primitives using basic modifiers such as Edit Mesh, Symmetry, Lathe and Sweep. Luckily many of the ornaments were repeated over and over in the scene, making my job much easier. Before anything else I set up the lighting using VRay planes – six of them to be exact, one at each window. They were set to be a bit smaller than the window frames in order to get sharper shadows. Later on they needed some adjustments, but the basic lighting setup was defined right here (**Fig.01a – b**).

The props – curtains, awnings, handles, vase and other elements – were all basic models. The shoes and the couch were not my own models, although the couch was modified to suit my needs; the shoes were modeled by my friend, Zsombor Gusztus,

Fig.01b

and the couch was originally modeled by Jesus Selvera. A noise modifier was added to the cushions to give them a more realistic feeling. I think it's really worth paying extra attention to the small details, like the placement of the shoes, the angle of the handles, the proper position of the camera and all the other little objects in the window. These elements will all help to increase the final image's overall atmosphere (**Fig.02**).

TEXTURING

In general, all materials had a dirt map in their diffuse slot with a different radius setting. For the couch I reused

© VIKTOR FRETYÁN

Fig.03

Fig.04

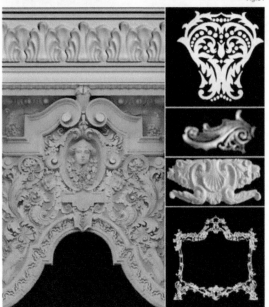

Fig.05

Fig.02

a shader from one of my previous scenes (**Fig.03**); it has a falloff material in the VRay dirt map's diffuse unoccluded slot, with Fresnel turned on ranging from dark brown to black (almost black – I never use 100 percent black!). For the bump and reflection I used the same bitmap (**Fig.04**) with the blur set to 0.1. The reflection was on Fresnel and the glossiness slot had the same map, but with a smaller percentage. The value of reflection glossiness was set to 0.86 and the highlight glossiness was set to 0.8.

The parquet flooring material was another interesting shader in the scene. For this one, I used different bitmaps for reflection, and bump, and the blur amount was set to 0.1. Reflection glossiness and highlight glossiness were also set differently here as well. I spent some time experimenting in order to get the right numbers for all the settings; it had to be perfect since it was the most relevant part of the scene.

The walls were given VRay dirt with a higher radius this time. The color was close to white and had a grayscale bitmap of a concrete surface in the reflection and bump slot set at a small value. Reflection glossiness was set to 0.75; for the small ornaments and decorations I used displacement modifiers on planes with 2D settings and various resolutions. These bitmaps were created by me using Photoshop on original photos (**Fig.05**).

Finally, the golden handles had a dirt map in the reflection slot with a small 2cm radius, and some bump was also given to them to achieve that rusted old look.

POST-PRODUCTION

After rendering the scene I did a lot of work in Photoshop until the image was finally complete. The first thing was a little balancing: there were some parts, mostly around the curtains, that were burnt, and some areas that were too dark. With some gamma adjustments and masking these problems were easily solved.

One of the most important things in order to create a desired atmosphere is to get the color balance right. The dark shades were increased a little towards the warm color tones, and the mid tones were moved towards the blue. I usually try out other variations and then decide which one to go with.

For the background, seen through the window, I used a photograph found on the internet. It needed some exposure, gamma and color corrections, as well as some distortion before it fitted the window scene perfectly. I then applied some Lens Blur to the bottom of the image to imitate a depth of field effect. And it was done! The difference after post-production is quite obvious compared with the original render, and it was achieved only by using basic Photoshop tools (**Fig.06**). In the final retouching I added some vignette, film grain and chromatic aberration using different plug-ins.

FINAL WORDS
As you can see, there was nothing extraordinary in the procedure. Technically, I am not that well trained and I have never really focused on that. I always believe that creating something valuable and beautiful in 3D is not necessarily a matter of technical achievements; the artists I truly admire – La Ke Hao and Alex Roman, for example – are outstanding because of their individual style and the atmosphere they create in their work. In this work of mine, I tried to impress the viewer with the simplest of tools.

Fig.06

ARTIST PORTFOLIO

OPEN GREEN
BY ANDRIUS BALCIUNAS

SOFTWARE USED: 3d Studio Max, ZBrush, Mental Ray and Photoshop

INTRODUCTION

It all started when I saw a simple photograph of a leaf lying on a hand. Because of the professional lighting of the image, or perhaps it was just my mood at the time, it just seemed so beautiful and pleasant. The green color of the leaf and the color of the skin suited each other so well, and it was this that really boosted my inspiration and motivated me to develop my own image. I wanted to create something glamorous yet also gentle, something easy to behold.

CONCEPT

I started the project using just two colors only, which I found to be an interesting approach. I simply began by painting with some simple soft brushstrokes, picking shades of cool greens and warm browns to develop the mood I wanted for the image (**Fig.01**). When I achieved something which resembled the mood I was looking for, I was sure that the final result was going to be satisfying as long as I kept the mood unchanged.

I already knew at the time that I wanted to create a girl dressed in green, and when I started to think about accessorizing her outfit with lots of chains and jewels

Fig.01

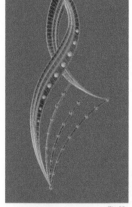

Fig.02a

Fig.02b

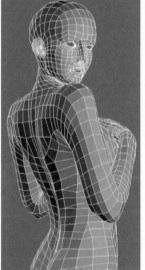

Fig.03

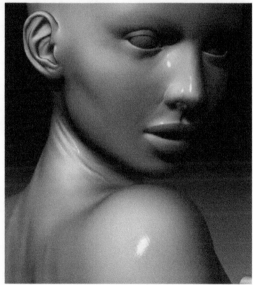

Fig.04

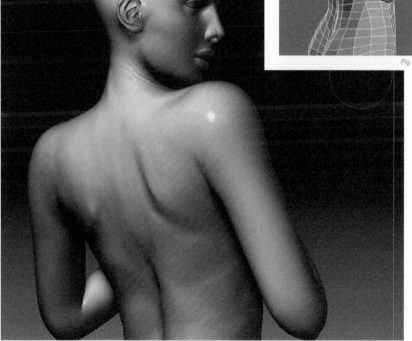

Fig.05

(**Fig.02a – b**), I came up with the idea of making a large glass ball as a pendant dangling down her back. It was at this very point that the title of the image came to me rather naturally: *Open Green*.

MODELING

I started collecting references of various girls on the internet, and found one photo in particular of the fashion model, Adriana Karembeu, very inspiring. She's really stunning, and I decided I wanted to create a CG model to have a similar beauty.

I started as usual with my "default" low poly base mesh, which I modify with each new project to suit my needs. I rigged the model with a biped and started to pose her as I desired, using references to achieve a natural posture

(**Fig.03**). I tweaked the pose, changed some of the proportions and fixed the model where it was necessary. This stage was critical and I probably spent most of the time right here. I was also working on a very old laptop at this part of the process because I was away on vacation, so when I got back home I took her into ZBrush to add further details and make some anatomical corrections (**Fig.04 – 06**). I wanted her to look natural, as well as very beautiful (**Fig.07**).

Making the cloth drape across her arms and around her back was a very interesting part of the process, and I probably wouldn't mention it if it hadn't turned out as well as it did. I started off thinking about sculpting it, but then decided to do a simulation instead to get a more natural look to the cloth. The main issue with this was

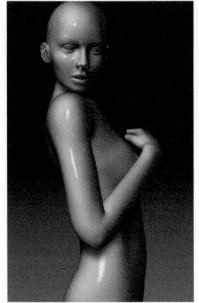

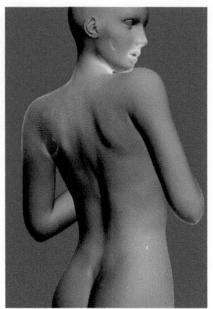

Fig.06

Fig.07

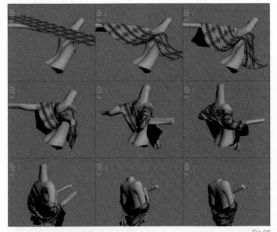

Fig.08

Fig.09

that her body needed to "catch" the cloth in order for it to naturally simulate on the model, so to get around this I basically made a morph between the "catch" pose and the original pose (**Fig.08**). I needed to tweak a lot of the morph's timing and the simulation parameters, but what I achieved as the end result was a natural looking, perfectly unwrapped cloth. This part was also done on my laptop, and because of this I had to optimize a model in order to make the simulations quicker for the previews. To finish up this cloth simulation, I tweaked it and added some minor details.

The chains were made using splines as paths for instant geometry chains. This technique worked out perfectly for me (**Fig.09 – 10**).

For the hair I used the Ornatrix plugin (I personally prefer this to the hair integrated in 3d Studio Max) (**Fig.11**). This was the last time I used this plugin for rendering hair

Fig.10

CHARACTERS

though, because it proved to have poor compatibility with Mental Ray, and I ended up having to render it separately with the Scanline renderer, which then caused me some trouble when I was in the compositing stage of the image creation. And whilst on the subject of her hair, I had an alternative idea for her to wear her hair loose, but I ended up leaving this idea behind and opting for the pinned up style, as it didn't look very interesting when worn down.

TEXTURING

When I started unwrapping the model I had a fixed perspective, so I decided to unwrap her so that none of the seams would be seen by the camera (**Fig.12**). This eliminated the problem of texture blending the seams, and before I started painting the skin textures, I first configured a skin shader (**Fig.13**). I then started to paint tones of color for her skin and makeup, detailing the skin with various brushes to imply imperfections and give the texture more realistic qualities (**Fig.14 – 16**).

The cloth texture was made by mixing a mask, a glossy reflective shader, and a standard shader with a falloff,

Fig.11

Fig.12

Fig.13

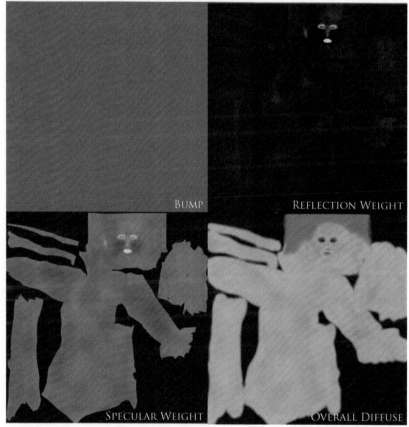

BUMP   REFLECTION WEIGHT

SPECULAR WEIGHT   OVERALL DIFFUSE

Fig.14

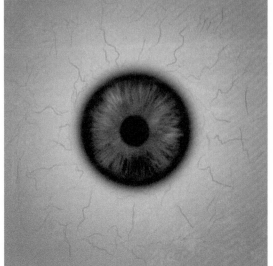

Fig.15

to mimic the look of cloth. I also used an opacity map for some areas to give a feeling of "lightness" to the cloth itself. The texture was painted using various patterns, mixing them together and applying different kaleidoscope effects to achieve something I felt worked. It was pretty much procedural, so I could easily make any mask from it if I needed to (**Fig.17a – c**).

LIGHTING

As usual I was expecting a lot of trouble when I came to the lighting, but luckily, this time, it all went smoothly. I used two photometric lights for my scene: a standard key light and back light setup. Since I was pretty happy with almost the very first render test, I decided to go deeper by exploring photometric light properties – particularly the web distribution parameters. I downloaded a whole pack of IES files from lithonia.com and started to experiment … I got some interesting results and noticed that some of the complex lighting distribution affected the rendering time – which was slower. I didn't go with anything too "extreme", I simply picked one that was almost like a default sphere web. The difference was that it was pleasingly affective in the decay of light. I also used a few planes in the scene as reflectors for the GI, to make the overall atmosphere a little warmer (**Fig.18 – 19**).

RENDERING & COMPOSITING

Before rendering the final image I removed all of the geometry parts that weren't visible to my fixed camera because they consumed virtual memory and I didn't want to include

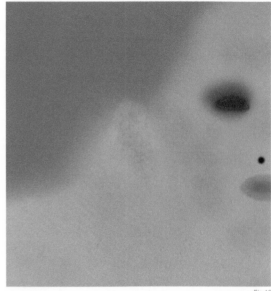
Fig.16

COLOR (FALLOFF SHADING)
Fig.17a

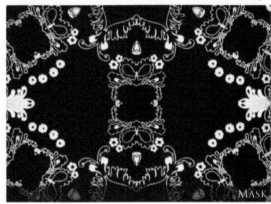
MASK
Fig.17b

OPACITY
Fig.17c

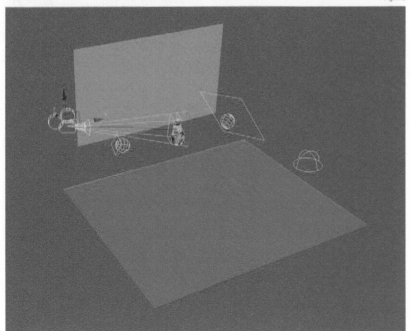
Fig.18

any needless calculations. I then split the rendering process into two sections: the hair as one part and everything else as the other. The whole rendering time for the full resolution render was around 18 hours.

When I was rendering the hair I used geometry just for the matte effect; I knew I couldn't do anything properly with shadows, so I had to configure the shader of the hair very accurately so it would look blond, whilst at the same time slightly affected by shadows. I used some noise maps for that effect.

When I was compositing everything together I also faked a slight shadow cast on her forehead and tweaked the overall color and contrast of her hair to better match everything. I also rendered a ZDepth pass to simulate the depth of field. And I ended up with four render passes which I then composed together in Photoshop (**Fig.20**).

CONCLUSION

Right from the very beginning of this project through to its end, I enjoyed the process of creation, particularly as it turned out to be so different from my usual workflow. It was a great experience for me and I'm very pleased with the final result.

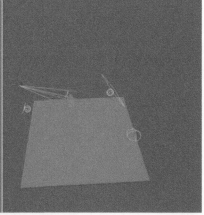
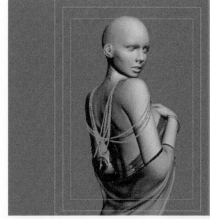

Fig.19

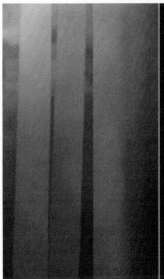

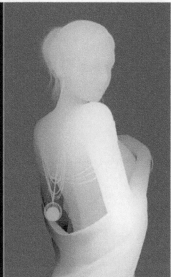

Fig.20

ARTIST PORTFOLIO

THE PORTRAIT OF A BISHOP
BY BRUNO MELO DE SOUZA

SOFTWARE USED: Softimage XSI, 3d Studio Max, ZBrush and Photoshop

INTRODUCTION

My main goal with the creation of this portrait was to test my modeling, texturing and compositing skills. The idea for the illustration started when I was looking for a slightly more original theme, with the possibility of creating a sensitive piece – perhaps an image that would prompt others to ask, "Why did the artist create this?" They might also wonder whether it's just a simple portrait, or if I was trying to send any messages … Some work can make others reflect on the theme, and so after some quick research I decided to go for a religious, or sacred, theme. I thought it would be a nice subject matter in which to try to achieve my goals.

Once my theme was set, I could focus on how to explore the subject. I knew that I wanted the exercise to push my skills, but I also wanted to create something relatively quick and simple, because my spare time was a little short. So after some further research, I found my perfect inspiration: portraits by the Masters such as Delacroix and Goya. Setting myself the task of creating a portrait with these goals, and without a lot of time to spare (I created this piece in two weeks during my free time) the work was a new and different experience for me.

MODELING

For the modeling, I began with an old bust model that I'd created for a previous project from a simple ZSphere.

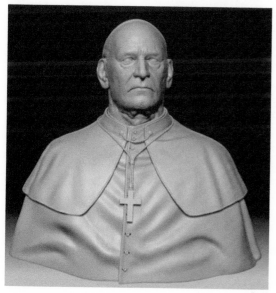

Fig.03

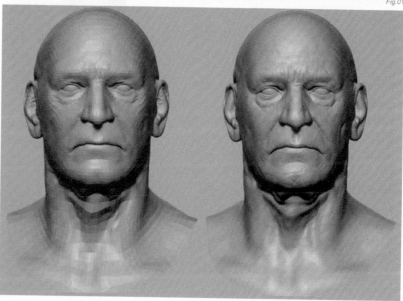

Fig.01

Fig.02

In ZBrush, I retopologized the base mesh with edgeloops, and modified and sculpted until I reached the result I was looking for (**Fig.01**). It was very important for me to make these changes at a low level of subdivision, because it's much easier to get the volumes and proportions right this way. To work on the smaller details I subdivided the mesh further (**Fig.02**), continuing to subdivide as I worked towards the wrinkles and other fine details. To me, this is the most efficient workflow and gives me more control over the stages of sculpting.

The cloth was just a simple base mesh made in Softimage XSI, which I then exported to ZBrush to get more detail. When all the work on the model was done (**Fig.03**), I exported a medium resolution mesh as my final and used a normal map to bring in all the small details (also created in ZBrush). I didn't worry about some technical modeling assets, such as refining edge loops or the final mesh resolution; it's nice not to have to waste time on things that will not appear or be used in a simple still, and in the case of this image I could simply focus on the modeling for just one image, without losing a lot of time.

UV MAPS, TEXTURES & MATERIALS

For the head, I used UV Layout in Softimage XSI to create a clean, fast and simple UV map; for the other pieces I used ZBrush to make a rougher, but very fast and effective UV map. And with my UVs ready, it was time to work on the textures.

I researched photographs of existing people to use as a base texture for the head, but before I could use them it was important to make some adjustments, such as removing unwanted reflections and any dirt from the photos. I find it interesting to make adjustments to get a cleaner feel to the photos, and also to find good colors from them to use for the base color for my model (I used a plugin called Image Plane to do this job quickly). The next step was to add more details – imperfections, saturated areas – always using lots of references to guide me. References of aged skins were particularly helpful in order to get the most realistic results (**Fig.04**).

After making some tests I realized that I didn't need to make specular and reflection maps; I just had to work hard on the procedurals to get a good result. I chose to use SSS Fast Skin Material (Mental Ray render system) and made several render tests to achieve a nice integration with just a simple color map as the "printed map", and a good specular and reflection. With good settings on materials, plus good control over the render passes, you can really improve the final result!

LIGHTING, RENDERING & POST-PRODUCTION

The lighting was quite simple: I used one Spot light for the main light, two Omni lights, and another Spot light for some rim light, with final gathering and an HDRI map on a sphere for the environmental lighting and reflections

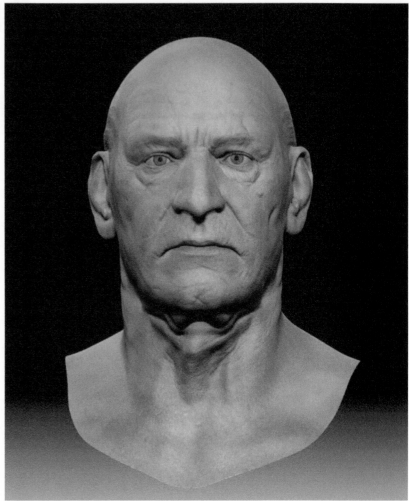

Fig.04

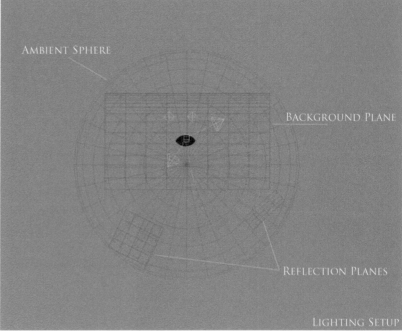

AMBIENT SPHERE

BACKGROUND PLANE

REFLECTION PLANES

LIGHTING SETUP

Fig.05

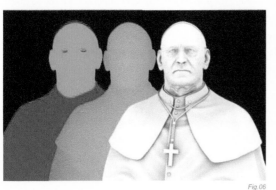

Fig.06

(**Fig.05**). I didn't go for any dramatic lighting at this stage because I wanted the work to be more focused on the creation of a realistic portrait (plus I wanted to add some drama to the lighting in post-production).

CHARACTERS

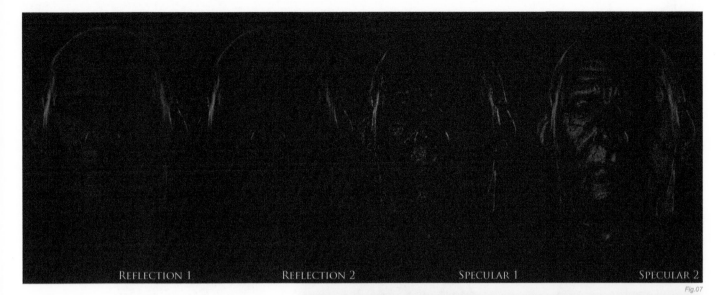

REFLECTION 1   REFLECTION 2   SPECULAR 1   SPECULAR 2

Fig.07

To me, working with separate render passes is very useful, because I can control each element individually. For example, I can adjust the intensity of some reflections and colors, or I can remove any unwanted specular. Using this method, I rendered out occlusion, reflection, specular, color and light passes, and composited them all in Photoshop (**Fig.06 – 08**).

CONCLUSION

Working on this character was great fun, and I believe that's important in order to keep up motivation on a project. I learned a lot throughout the process, mostly in the texture, lighting and rendering stages. There are of course some things I would like to change, or perhaps do some tests to try and get a better result, but I am generally very pleased with the final image. I reached the initial goals I set for myself; I feel more prepared now to do more and more challenging work, always aiming to create better results than the last.

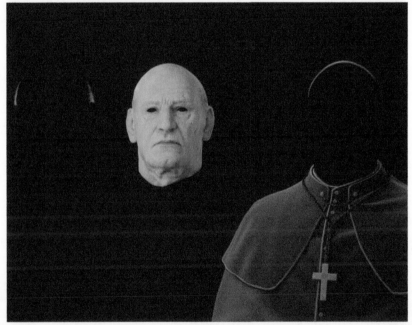

Fig.08

ARTIST PORTFOLIO

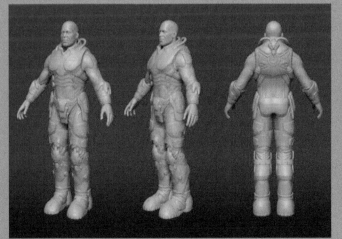

SARKHAN VOL
By Daarken

SOFTWARE USED: Photoshop

CONCEPT

Planeswalkers are some of the most important illustrations in *Magic: The Gathering*. Not only are they essential to the storyline, but they also represent an iconic look for the Magic multiverse. I was very excited to have the privilege of creating Sarkhan Vol for the "Shards of Alara" set. Sarkhan Vol is a multicolored red and green card, which means I am going to need to have some red and green elements in the illustration. The idea behind Sarkhan Vol is that he is a shaman who spends his life in search of dragons – not to kill them, but to pay them homage.

Fig.01

Fig.02

Fig.03

GETTING STARTED

Usually when I start an illustration I have a vague idea of what I want to paint, but most of my ideas develop while I'm painting. People usually call these "happy accidents". I like to call it "an artist who isn't sure what he is doing but ends up finding something amidst the chaos and pretends he knows what he is doing". I think that's why I don't start out with any line drawings or preliminary sketches. I like to just dive in and find things in the random shapes that I paint. I'm sure my process tends to give my art directors heartburn and headaches. Luckily they trust me enough to let me run with my ideas.

Since Sarkhan Vol is going to be a green/red card, I decided that I would put him in a mountainous environment that fades to green towards the horizon (**Fig.01**). My painting process varies all the time. Sometimes I start in color while other times I start in black and white, depending on whether I have a strong idea of what I want the final illustration to look like. Color is usually one of the hardest parts of an illustration for me. I choose to start in black and white so that I don't waste too much time sitting around thinking about what kind of color scheme to do. I always keep things very loose in the beginning; this allows me to focus on composition and silhouettes, as opposed to details. After I get those things working fairly well I start the refining process.

My first idea was to show Sarkhan Vol looking up into the sky with a look of awe and reverence for the dragons flying overhead (**Fig.02**). Within the past year I began drawing in line instead of painting silhouettes during the early part of my paintings. The reason for this is that it allows the art director to understand the painting more at an earlier stage. I think it also helps to deter me from painting too darkly, forcing me to paint from light to dark instead of dark to light.

At this stage I'm only worried about the pose and hinting at the character design (**Fig.03**). I try and work all over the canvas; this helps me avoid getting bogged down too much on any particular area and also helps me visualize what the final illustration will look like. I also work zoomed out so that I can see the entire canvas. This way I can see how the separate elements relate to each other in the composition. I would say I probably work zoomed out for a good 80% of the illustration and only zoom in for the final details. Working this way helps me to see my errors more easily and also lets me work faster. Early on I like to keep the figure on a separate layer from the background. Keeping the figure separate makes it easier for me to change the pose, which I know I will change several times before I settle on something that I like.

Fig.04

Already I am starting to play around with different poses (**Fig.04**). The beauty of working digitally is that I can make these changes easily and take more chances without the fear of having to start over. Now that I have something that I am fairly happy with, I can start refining the shapes (**Fig.05**). Adding light behind the focus pulls it out; it gives the painting more depth and causes an area of high contrast which will draw the attention of the viewer.

Sarkhan Vol looks a little weak and timid, so I need to make him look stronger. Pulling the shoulders back and puffing out his chest will make him appear more confident and give him a more commanding presence (**Fig.06**). I also added some more lava around his feet to add more interest near the bottom of the canvas. The lava will also help to add some reflected light to the floating rocks. I wanted to add the floating rocks to hint at Sarkhan Vol's magical abilities just bubbling under the surface. At this stage I am ready to submit my sketch for review.

Fig.05

CHARACTERS

Fig.06

CHANGES

The feedback I received was that I needed to put Sarkhan Vol in a more dynamic pose. He also needed to connect to the viewer a bit more. I also had to lose the skulls and the dragon-headed pauldron. Luckily I still had Sarkhan Vol on a separate layer, so I quickly roughed in another pose, one where Sarkhan Vol is facing the viewer with outstretched arms as if he is allowing his love for dragons to wash over him, bringing him to the point of ecstasy (**Fig.07**). I wasn't really happy with this pose, so I scrapped it and started over.

ADDING COLOR

I decided to go with a more engaging and confrontational pose (**Fig.08**). Now that I have the new pose established I can start with color. One of the big misconceptions about digital work is that people tend to have the belief that the computer does everything for you. Adding color isn't just a simple button click or one all-powerful filter, it is a slow process that utilizes many layer types as well as opaque painting. I add the base colors on a new layer that I set to Overlay. I tend to use either Overlay or Hard Light to add color to my paintings. Some of the light areas in the background are painted opaquely on a layer above the overlay layer.

THE UGLY PHASE

The ugly phase is the most intimidating stage of all. All of my paintings go through what I call "The Ugly Phase".

Fig.07   Fig.08

Fig.09

This is the stage in which I am still trying to block in shapes and correct my drawing. At this point I am more interested in getting things down on canvas, as opposed to making them look pretty, because I know I can go back later and fix things (**Fig.09**). Many times I reach this phase and stop, believing that it looks too terrible to continue. My confidence level always takes a severe blow at this stage and requires a tremendous amount of willpower to push on. If you ever reach this phase just keep at it, things will start to evolve and fall into place.

LIFE AFTER THE UGLY

There are so many errors right now it's ridiculous (**Fig.10**). He has no neck, his right arm is missing a forearm, his left arm is too big, and his legs are too short. My process is a constant battle of pushing and pulling shapes, beating them into submission until they work.

Fig.10

Since I have my base colors in place I can start playing around with the color balance (**Fig.11a**). The easiest way to use color balance is to add an adjustment layer. This way you are making the color changes on a separate layer instead of changing your actual painting. Click on the half black, half white circle (**Fig.11b**). A dialog box comes up with a list of adjustment and fill layers to choose from. First I choose Hue/Saturation and increase the saturation by 8. On top of that I create a color balance layer that adds more red, magenta and yellow.

One thing to keep in mind while working is to take a break every so often. Looking at your illustration with fresh eyes can cause errors to become more apparent. You might also see some things that you can add or remove. Flipping the image horizontally can also help you see things in a new light. I realize here that the upper

Fig.11a

Fig.11b

Fig.13

Fig.12

half of his body is too big, and his lower half too small (**Fig.12**). I am also still changing the colors and refining the shapes and design. At this point I add a texture layer on another layer set to Overlay (**Fig.13**). I also change the opacity of the texture layer to 30%. After I have the texture layer in I start painting opaquely on top of it. I want to add more blue to his skin color now, so I select his body with the Lasso tool (**Fig.14**). After I have my selection I hit Ctrl + Shift + C to copy all layers, then Ctrl

+ V to paste. I can then hit Ctrl + B to open the color balance dialog box. You can then easily erase the parts you didn't want to change. Once again I change his skin color by adding more magenta (**Fig.15a**). I also lengthen his arms and torso.

Usually when I paint I don't push the contrast enough, so I go back with Color Dodge. For the skin I select the area and hit Ctrl + Shift + C, then Ctrl + V. Select the brush tool and then change the brush properties to Color Dodge (**Fig.15b**). By selecting a darker color I can gradually bring up the color and contrast without overexposing it too quickly. I would also recommend using a soft brush, like the airbrush.

I originally had **Fig.15a** as the final illustration, but after coming back and looking at it I made some changes, such as shortening his legs and adding some strands of hair in front of his face (**Fig.16**). Most of the time you never really finish an illustration – you simply run out of time!

Fig.14

Fig.15a

Fig.15b

Fig.16

Closing

Going into this project I had a lot of pressure to live up to since Aleski Briclot illustrated the previous Planeswalkers. I'm not sure if I accomplished the goal of creating a Planeswalker cool enough to stand next to Aleksi's, but I had a lot of fun working on it. Hopefully Sarkhan Vol can continue his trek through the primordial lands of Jund, in search of a dragon worthy of his worship.

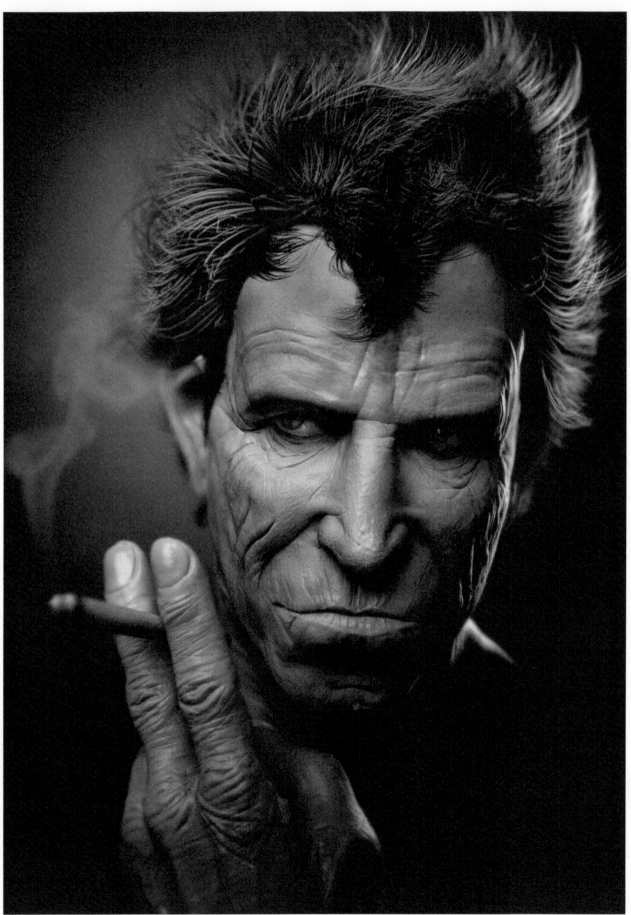

PORTRAIT OF KEITH RICHARDS
BY JELMER BOSKMA

SOFTWARE USED: Softimage XSI, ZBrush and Photoshop

INTRODUCTION

It all started in a Vancouver theatre around May 2007 where I watched the third part of the *Pirates of the Caribbean: At World's End* for the first time. About half way in, Keith Richards made his introduction in the role of Captain Teague. When he appeared on screen I had goose bumps; the way Keith looked in his red pirate costume reminded me so much of an illustration of the infamous pirate, Blackbeard, in a children's pirate book I used to own – I loved that image and have kept it in my head ever since. A few months later, Disney released the book *The Art of the Pirates of the Caribbean* where I once again met with Captain Teague. This time he appeared in the form of an amazing drawing done by one of my heroes, Mark "Crash" McCreery. There the idea was born.

I felt it was time to add something new to my portfolio, and this would be something I'd very much enjoy doing. Although I started off with the intent to create a portrait of Keith Richards as Captain Teague, he never made it to that state. I changed my mind during the process and decided to go for a realistic portrait of the man himself instead. Well … at least it got me a good "piratey" introduction for this article – Yarr!

REFERENCES

I started off the way I usually start any project, which is by gathering related reference imagery. I found a couple

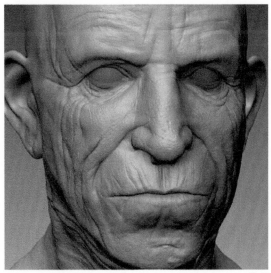

Fig.02

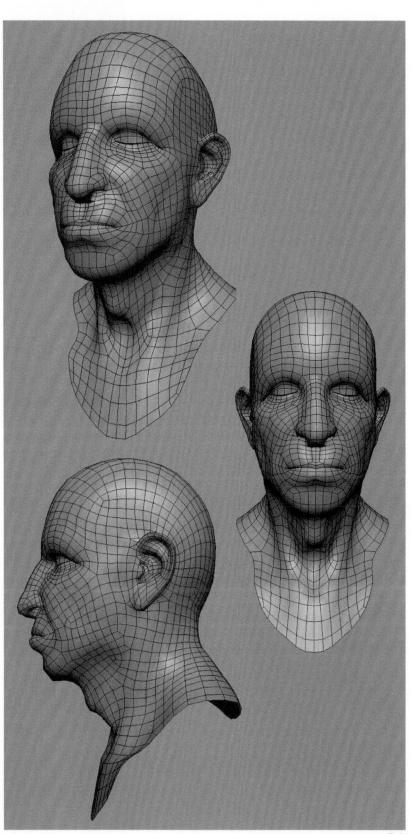

Fig.01

of decent photos of Keith and also took some screen grabs from the movies, where I had the opportunity to see him from more specific angles. During my search for references it was inevitable that I came across some of the famous caricaturist, Sebastian Krueger's work. He has portrayed and caricaturized the Rolling Stones, and Keith personally, quite a few times. Throughout the process I constantly had to be aware not to caricaturize my portrait too much. Keith has got a lot of characterizing features in his face, and sticking close to his real proportions, instead of caricaturizing them, was a challenge!

MODELING

I mocked up a base mesh for the bust in XSI fairly quickly, with the idea to get working on the likeness in ZBrush as soon as possible. I kept the base model very simple, since it would be used for still purposes only, and wouldn't have to deform (**Fig.01**).

SCULPTING

When doing a likeness, details hardly matter; it's the main proportions that matter, and in particular the visual triangle indicating the relations between the eyes and tip of the nose. I found that once you nail those proportions, the character usually starts to become recognisable. You do start to stare blind after a certain amount of time, so I tried to get as much of the main work done as possible within the first hours after starting work on the model.

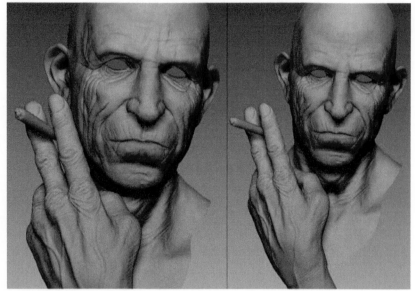

Fig.03

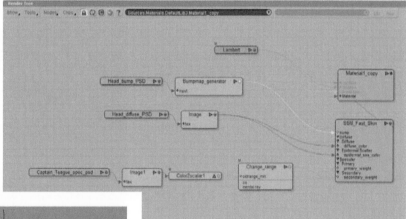

Fig.04

I tend to start off by subdividing the model about three times right after importing it into ZBrush. From there I start to refine and build the main forms. I have become a big fan of the Clay Tubes tool, which allows me to change and add volume in certain areas in a very natural way. After getting the bigger primary forms down I carved in a couple of Keith's most characterizing wrinkles, which are formed mostly around his mouth and cheekbones. Having a dual monitor setup was most helpful for this project: I find that being able to have my main reference images up on one screen, while working on the other, is almost mandatory for this kind of work. Once I started sculpting it was just a matter of constant refinement: looking at the reference photos and comparing them to the model. I didn't really find any shortcuts or tricks doing a portrait – it seems to be just a matter of training your eye and trying to sculpt what you can see (**Fig.02 – 03**).

TEXTURING & SHADING

The texture painting was completely done in ZBrush as well. Using the polypaint tools I quickly painted a diffuse

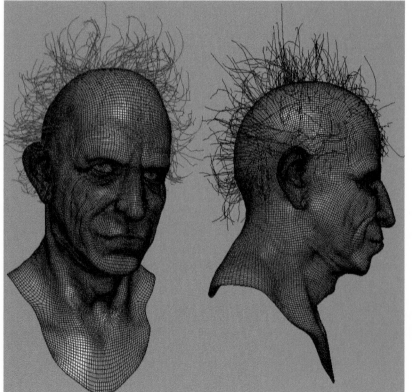

Fig.05

texture directly on the model. Knowing the final image would be black and white, I didn't spend too much time on this.

After having exported the diffuse map from ZBrush, I hooked the image up in a pretty simple shading tree using Mental Ray's standard fast skin surface shader (**Fig.04**). I applied this to the high-res model, right out of ZBrush. The model sits at about 2 million quad polygons at its highest subdivision level, and I sadly wasn't able to render this in XSI without crashing my machine. I ended up exporting the second highest resolution mesh and generating an additional map, based on the volume differences between the highest two levels and applied this as a bump map to the model in XSI.

HAIR

The hair was done in XSI, too – the hair tools are great and pretty easy to use. I grew about eight different selections of hair to form his haircut. I looked at sections

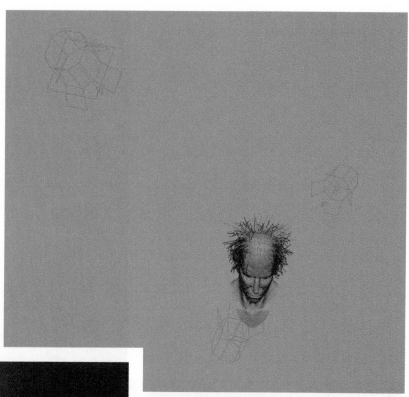

Fig.06

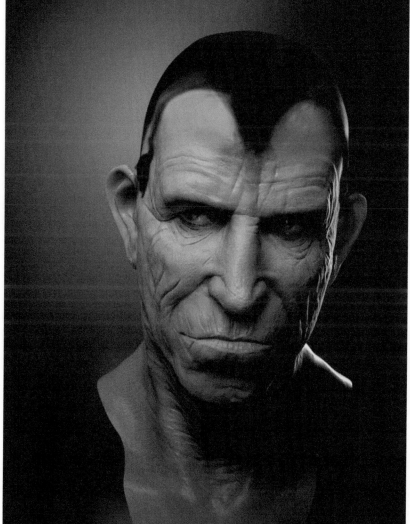

Fig.07a

Fig.07b

and strands that characterized his hair most to base my hair selections on, and focused on those specific areas. The hair was very much modeled to the camera, and looks rather ridiculous from any other angle (**Fig.05**).

LIGHTING & RENDERING

The final light rig was made up out of a standard three-point light setup using area-lights. The key light was placed on a sharp angle high above the model to create deep shadows under his eyebrows – something I found to help sell the likeness a bit more. A bright rim light was placed directly behind Keith, to separate him from the background a little. To soften out some of the shadows on one side and generate some nice contrast in the lighting, I placed a soft fill light on the left side of the model (**Fig.06**).

The image was rendered in 4 passes, those being two specular and beauty passes for the head and the hand plus the cigarette. The beauty pass showed the model lit and fully shaded, but without any specular highlights. Those were rendered out separately in a specular pass, so that I could have a bit more control over it later on in Photoshop.

COMPOSITING & FINALIZING

There wasn't too much work left to be done in Photoshop besides combining all the passes, desaturating the image, adjusting the levels a touch and adding a depth of

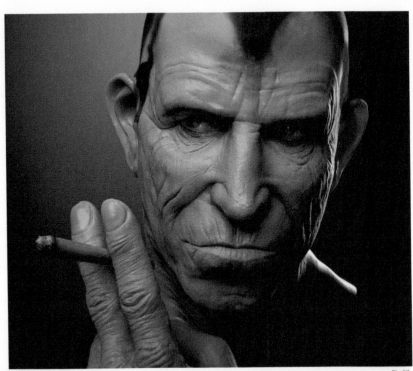

Fig.07c

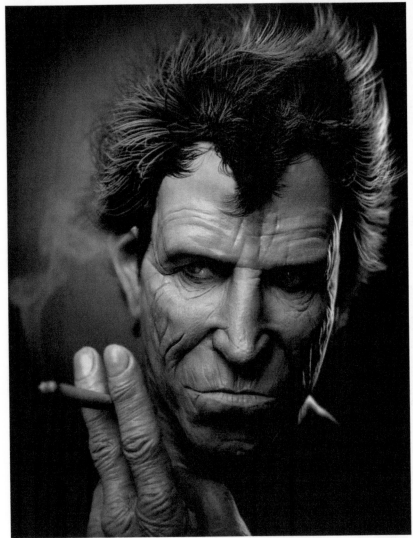

Fig.07e

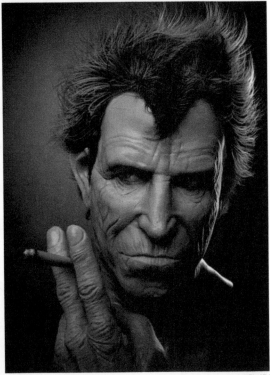

Fig.07d

field effect using the blur tools. The smoke was painted in later, and to finish the whole thing off I added some grain, which I found added a lot of character to the final image (**Fig.07a – e**).

CONCLUSION

And that's about it! I very much enjoyed working on this portrait and am happy to call this one done. I hope you like it.

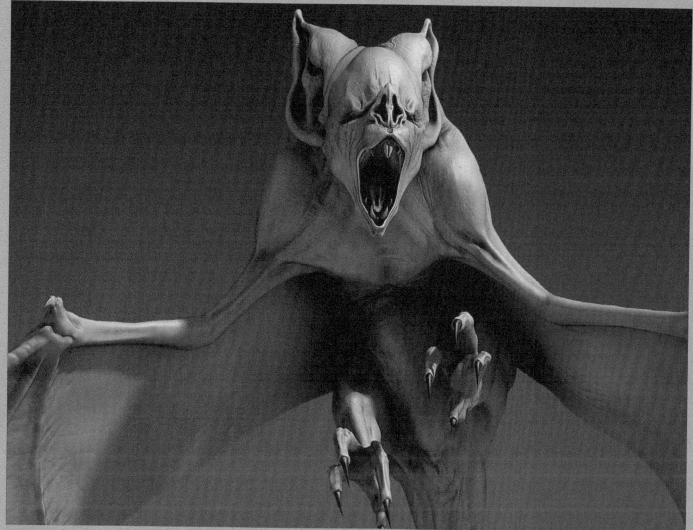

© Jelmer Boskma 2006

© Jelmer Boskma 2006

© Jelmer Boskma 2007

© Jelmer Boskma 2008

GOING CALIFORNIA
BY LOÏC E338 ZIMMERMANN

SOFTWARE USED: Maya, ZBrush, Mental Ray and Photoshop

INTRODUCTION

It's all been said, all been explained over and over, I guess – how you start from a low-res mesh, to end up sculpting millions of polygons and rendering the stuff out with fancy candle shaders. When I was told my image would be part of this book, joy was my first feeling … quickly followed by a sudden fear: it's all been said before. So instead of the usual approach, I'll try a different take here in order to explain "why", instead of "how", since you should already know how.

My illustration work relies on 3D (although it's changing) since I find myself more comfortable with it for "ideation" (as they call it in concept art) compared to drawing (due to a shameful lack of practice). Most of the time I go for a radical approach and it takes only a few hours to get my character done; it's simple and not textured, but good enough to get started with Photoshop and Painter to end up with, hopefully, something very natural and 2D-ish. Once in a while, I push the 3D side farther in order to end up with a very detailed image, closer to a photographical approach.

Fig.01b

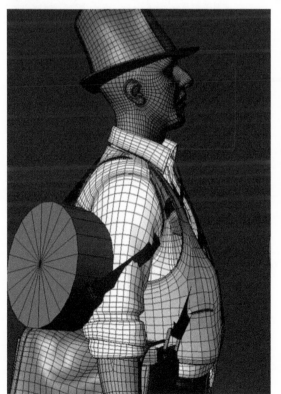

Fig.01a

Fig.02

I wanted to celebrate my upcoming journey into the US, due to a recent job proposal in Venice, California. I thought it would be interesting to make the parallel with those European colonials who took the journey in the late 19th Century, hoping for a piece of gold (although these days the picture isn't the same and the economy is crumbling). Anyway! I took my digital double from the *Longmen's Fall* project (featured in *Digital Art Masters: Volume 3*) and dressed him up to make this portrait, choosing not to go for the pure sepia feeling, although it is always charming, but sticking to a colored image – more Western, so to speak.

FEED THE MACHINE!

Before you even start, especially when dealing with a subject related to history, you must spend some time gathering references. I basically searched for suitcase designs, leather objects, monocles ... just a few items, since the look of the guy wasn't meant to be fancy. Regular clothes, regular accessories; I wanted things to remain simple, and while doing the parallel with the gold rush it had to take place now. The vest was the only "urban" item, as well as the shape of the hat. The pants and the shirt are both very neutral.

I used some temp assets that already existed to create the shirt, pants, vest and hat. The beauty of CG is in building a bank of assets you can reuse, tweak, improve combine – whatever. I hate having to start from scratch (over the years I've lost patience – it's a fact). Anyway, thanks to this method I was able to come up with all that was not flesh in two days or so for the base mesh (the project was done at night). Texturing took a while, but after a year and a half spent on *Heavy Rain* (a PS3 video-game from Quantic Dream), I had some practice and it went smoothly. Plus it was a joy not to be limited by a game engine and able to use 4- and 6K textures!

Having a bank of assets is also a very good thing when you want to deal with textures. UV-mapping is always kind of a hassle, and I like having a good starting point

Fig.03

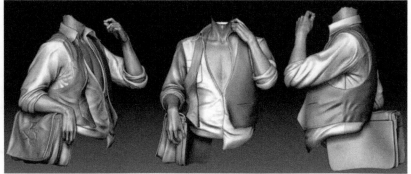

Fig.04

Fig.05

on all my geometry before I start refining. This gives you a very good base for unwrapping stuff quickly when the tweaking is over.

CLOTHING & PROPS

I kept the modeling very simple within Maya, knowing that all the fabric would be done in ZBrush anyway (**Fig.01a – b**). When I had all the elements in the scene, I exported them as .obj files for further sculpting. The initial global sculpting was done in a day. The pose was achieved using Transpose and SubTool master. It's a convenient way when one doesn't want to deal with rigging and skinning, but it's a bit tedious for anyone who has had the chance to play with a nice IK/FK rig!

When the posing was achieved, I made an additional pass of sculpting to create some matching folds and wrinkles (**Fig.02 – 03**). The leather bag is actually mine (**Fig.04**); I thought it was good to include some contemporary elements in the image, and references for it were easy to get. I took pictures of it for modeling

Fig.06

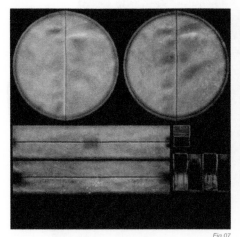

Fig.07

Fig.08

Fig.09

and texturing purposes, using an indirect and diffuse "daylight" to avoid sharp specular highlights.

Once the modeling was done I made a compact UV layout (all elements related to the bag in one layout) and started to copy and paste photos onto it. Using the Stamp and the Healing brush tool I filled in all the gaps and fixed the specular highlights. Using the Liquify filter I tweaked the texture so it matched my UVs perfectly. Then I painted details on top and generated additional textures (spec, bump). This same method was used for all the objects (**Fig.05 – 06**).

It's important to put some love into the details of your textures (**Fig.07 – 09**). Breaking the edges with a specular highlight is a good start – think of what it's like in the real world. You can then say yes, this is because the surface is softer, or glossier, and then you can update the diffuse and bump accordingly. Experience of videogame texturing is a very good thing, since you have to pay a lot of attention to your textures, with simple shaders on top and size limitations. You often have to force things a bit so they work under most conditions. For rendered projects you have to be careful not to overdo it too much, but still, it's good to help the shader a bit!

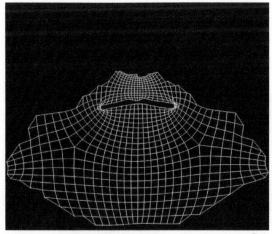

Fig.11

Fig.10

THE HEAD

The face I did for the *Longmen's Fall* image was alright, but I wanted to add a little more aging to it. Since the character has a hat and some hair I ended up cutting a mask into the face in order to reach a higher poly count. Since the head was attached to the torso and arms I was limited to a global 5 million polygons. By doing this I was able to reach the 5 million I needed on the face alone. My computer tends to crash beyond that (**Fig.10**).

Initially I wanted to have a pure, traditional sculpted feel to the beard. There were two reasons to this – the first being that it's cool, and as much as I dislike those CG copies of classical pieces there are some fantastic things happening in old school sculpting that are very inspirational. What I mean is: copying a real sculpture with digital tools is a piece of cake compared with what it was to practically do; I just find it a bit hypocritical. The second reason is because fur is another thing I hate doing. So I had to open the gates of hell and go for the fur. Laziness shall always bow down to the necessities of an image! The sculpting approach couldn't render the fuzzy feel I needed to fit in with the elements already composing the picture (which were pretty realistic). But at least it helped with giving a solid base to the fur, and it was really fun doing it.

I extracted emitters from the geometry of the face to make the fur work a bit easier (a matter of taste). This also allowed me to scale up the UVs and be able to use smaller textures for both colors and weight attributes (**Fig.11**). I baked the color of the face onto those new UVs since it had the beard painted already. This gave me a nice matching color that helped with integrating those damn hairs. I adjusted the color gain in Maya for specific attribute variations. This is usually fair enough (tip color vs. root color) and keeps the file tracking simple (**Fig.12**).

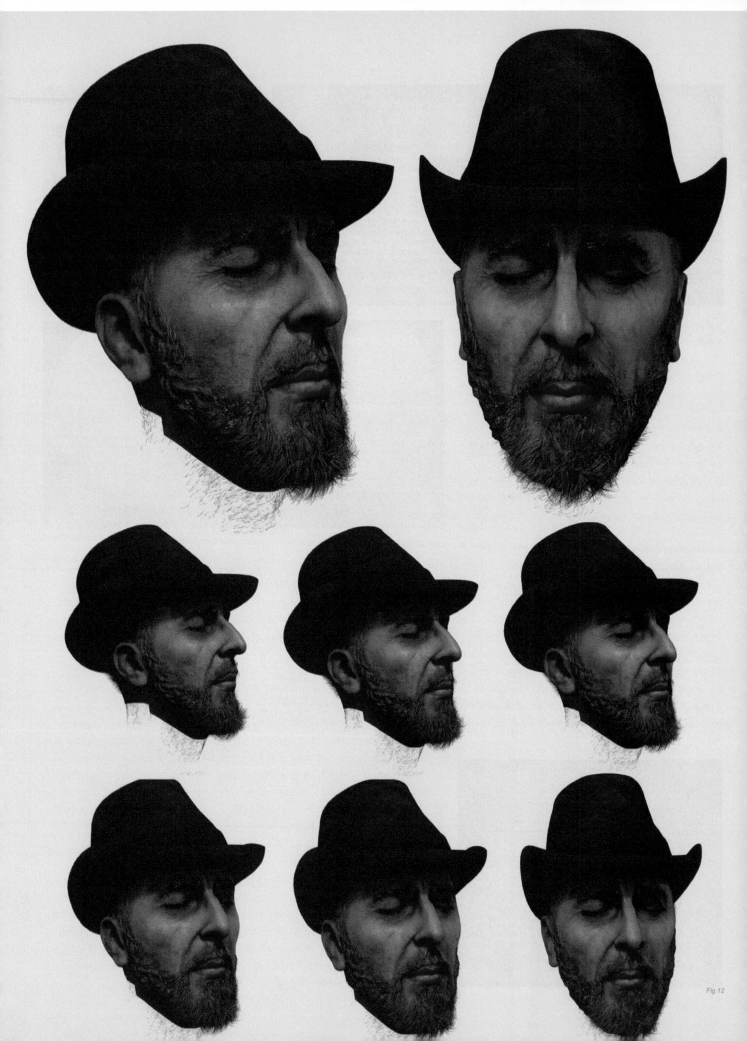

Fig.12

Fig.13

I ended up painting additional hair in Photoshop to make it look more convincing. Next time I'll skip the fur stage for real and jump directly to the painting. I understand the appeal of making it fully in 3D though – that little "playing God" thing that happens. But let's be serious, for creating just one image it just doesn't make sense at all!

ASSEMBLING PASSES

In the end I had something like 600MB of textures for this guy. If you add displacement for most of the elements and a naughty SSS of some elements and raytraced shadows, you have enough to scare any CPU to death! I was using 2K textures for my tests, but in the end it was the 4- and 6K that I wanted. So I broke the scene into passes: clothes, bags, body and face, monocle and hat, and the fur. I also rendered some additional passes for the specular, occlusion and HDRI. I ended up replacing some of the specs with some heavy reflections. Although it's obvious this was going to be better, I always try to see how far I can go with regular specular before choosing Raytrace. One could say it doesn't really show in the image (it could be improved – I'll give you that), but hey, it does the trick (**Fig.13**).

Although the close-ups with full-res textures I did were looking alright, when I had all the passes assembled in Photoshop for the first time, I realized the lighting was not good at all. The shaders were not as nice as they were with a simple direct lighting with HDRI. Their behavior in sharp lighting was as poor as it could be! But with only one day of work left in my schedule, I really had no time to redo it. At this point, I saw myself throwing the

Fig.14

Fig.15

computer through the window … but then I thought it might hurt one of my cats and decided to do my best with Photoshop.

Using adjustment layers on Levels and Hues first, I painted masks to push values in the highlights and the shadows, giving more "punch" to the image. A second set of adjustment layers was used to push the colors, giving more life to the character. The third round was made of textures, stains, scratches ... and some "discreet" paint-over. I added a quick matte painting for the background and tweaked my colors again so the whole thing worked together (**Fig.14 – 15**). The last two hours were used painting additional details, seams, tiny shadows, textures, hair …

… and we're done.

CONCLUSION

If you ask me now, I think the result is way too shy and I would go for something drastically different. I had to keep it quiet for the posing and this has been bugging me a bit. On the rendering side, something with much more contrast, dark shadows, straight from *Pale Rider* would be good as well. Considering the clothes, and since I'm really back into the 19th Century these days, I would go for a neat gentleman's shirt, pants and jacket, bruised by travel. But this is it: an exercise that turned out to be a nice experience, and gave me the chance to polish up some of my techniques.

This image is most likely one of the last of its kind. Texturing and shading no longer get my attention for personal work, but I still enjoy sculpting a lot. Lighting is also something that can be fast, and with those last two,

you've got a good half of the work done already. But it's good to go through all these steps and to learn, trying to get a global picture of 3D. It allows you to understand what the folks you work with are doing, and also helps you provide them with what they need before they have to ask. As a Lead or a Supervisor, it also helps not looking like an ass because you don't know what you're talking about!

It's also important to figure out what you really need, and then dig into all those and make them your own. They – the tools, the software – should always be a fast track between you and your finished concepts. It's good to get rid of any useless baggage … Is this the real story behind this picture? Well, I don't know; I left a lot behind me when I moved to California, for sure, but it doesn't feel any lighter at all (**Fig.16** – the remake).

Fig.16

BARBARIAN CHICK
BY MACIEJ KUCIARA

SOFTWARE USED: Photoshop

IDEA

The hardest thing in concept art and illustration production I find is getting an appealing idea that will sell the image. It doesn't matter if I'm creating a picture just for fun or for production purposes; I try to keep the workflow the same in both cases.

For this *Barbarian Chick* picture, I got some serious inspiration from both fantasy computer games as well as Frank Frazetta's masterpieces. The idea with this piece was pretty simple: create a hero type, a cool character that any potential gamer (if that piece would end up as conceptual image for game assets) could relate to. I thought confronting the fragility of beauty and barbaric gore would fulfill the idea perfectly! The major challenge I found with this image was to mix a painterly style with realistic rendering, but surprisingly it went pretty smoothly.

COMPOSITION

The first thing I do to settle my ideas down is to throw in some colors and create a composition that I might

Fig.01

be happy with. This step is really important for me, as it defines all the tools and requirements I will have to handle in order to create final the image.

I started roughly with shapes and colors (**Fig.01**) to define the composition, mood and brief idea that was hiding behind the artwork. I used a lot of different custom brushes and parts of old pictures that I had made before. The reason for this was to shorten the painting time and to find out if the idea that I had in my mind was really working. I personally think that figuring out if your ideas will work as you wish them to in a final image is something that will either make the painting process easy or painful. There are times when I do dozens of 5-10 minute doodles, or even very dirty and ugly photo collages, to prove to myself I'm doing something that will kick ass. In the *Barbarian Chick* image, there was just the one sketch for this piece, since the image itself wasn't really complicated in terms of the composition and idea. Beautiful barbarian girl + swords + blood = awesome!

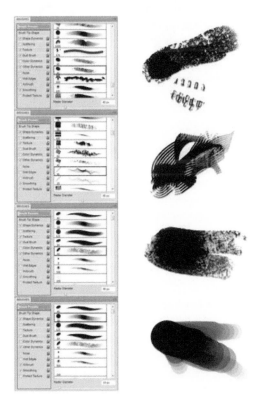

Fig.02

Colors

With every image I work on I try to ensure that I keep the color palette consistent from beginning to end. There is nothing more frustrating than refactoring an entire image with different color warmth when you're not happy with how the image looks. As I mentioned before, I always start with colorful doodles to convince and commit myself to the idea that I decide to work on. With *Barbarian Chick* I wanted to go with warm bloody colors with a complementary blue tint for the background and highlights. I can't count how many images I've scrapped and never got back to, just because the initial idea wasn't really well thoughtout. Thankfully, *Barbarian Chick* was one of those strong ideas I found really easy to follow.

Details

Once the idea is there, I start to examine the image briefly and try to figure out what kind of materials I will have to use to get all the details I want to achieve in the final image. For this particular image I knew I would need to work with realistic looking materials, such as fur, skin and armor. From that point of view, I always go through all the pictures I've created so far, as well as my custom brushes and textures (**Fig.02**). If I can't find a material there that I need, I either try to make it or use a good reference texture or image that will just make my life

Fig.03

SOURCE: HTTP://WWW.SXC.HU/PHOTO/623967

Fig.04

HTTP://WWW.NELSHAEL.COM

Fig.05

SOURCE: HTTP://WWW.SXC.HU/PHOTO/406969

Fig.06

SOURCE: CGTEXTURES.COM

Fig.07

easier. I avoid detailing things pixel by pixel at all costs, as it just takes too much time and kills productivity.

During the detail stage I also look at the bigger picture of the piece I'm working on. I try to figure out if there are any elements missing, or if adding something to the image will make it better or not. At this stage adding a dead body lying at the bottom of the composition was a nice addition to the beauty–gore mix (**Fig.03**).

On *Barbarian Chick* herself, I used three reference images: fur (**Fig.04**), for defining the brush pattern and color ranges for the chick's skirt and fur elements; leather armor (**Fig.05 – 06**), from which I cloned the leather pattern for the corset and straps; and pebbles (**Fig.07**), using a photo texture from cgtextures.com to detail out

CHARACTERS

Fig.08

the rock parts of the picture. The rest of the material I covered with brushes and texture layouts that I had used in other images created beforehand.

The only really difficult part of the main character was keeping her face rather realistic; as for the body, I made enough clothing shortcuts to get away with body proportions and anatomy. This is where the "gore" mix came in handy, since using cheap red body paint and blood splashes covered a lot of details that I didn't have to worry about, as well as brought in the idea that I wanted to achieve for this picture.

More gore and details

Once most details were in place, I noticed the picture was still missing some gore, or at least it wasn't quite "there yet", for me. The easiest way to gore-it-out was to add some blood splashes here and there. Since I didn't want to make it too random, but rather sit nicely in place and enhance the core idea for this picture, I decided to add a nasty blood splash, a sort of path connection, between the beautiful killer and her victim (**Fig.08 – 09**).

Once I was happy with it, I used custom brushes on the topmost layer with lower opacities, to connect all the pieces nicely together and to enhance the painterly look of the image (**Fig.10**). Blending sharper parts together is something that I use in my images quite often, since it's a

Fig.09

Fig.10

very cheap way to make an image more consistent, especially if you go with shortcuts, such as textures and photographic elements in your images.

Conclusion

There are those images that you finish off and you're happy with, and then there are others that you find working just "OK", but you still end up with mixed feelings, like you could have done better. *Barbarian Chick* was one of those images I found myself really happy with in the end, not just because I accomplished the goal I set up for myself, but also because at some point this picture became a good learning process. I've made my work library bigger with a few new custom brushes and some more painting experience, which is always good!

EXIT 411 WEST
Come on FFS!

THE SHIPWRECK
BY MARC BRUNET

SOFTWARE USED: Photoshop

INTRODUCTION
Most of the time my image-creation process is what could be called – with reason – "a mess". When I paint for myself, I stray from the normal and methodical work environment I put up with everyday of the week at the studio, and try to have some fun exploring new things. Even though this image was done for the prestigious and very British *ImagineFX* magazine in the first place, they gave me such freedom it felt like I was simply painting for myself.

We agreed pirates would be an interesting subject to explore, and since winter was approaching my brain just couldn't resist the temptation to draw something warm and tropical in a mere attempt to counter the actual cold temperature. Unfortunately, it didn't get any warmer. At least I tried.

The rest basically came into place by itself. Would there ever be anything more awesome than a pirate captain in a bikini? No. So there I had it: a pretty good idea of where I was going, subject-wise. For the rest I decided to focus

Fig.01

Fig.02

mainly on composition and challenge myself with it by including as many aspects as possible. Put on your shades – what follows will explain this tricky process.

PRINCIPLES
Composition in art is, most of the time, left behind and not paid much attention to. This is not a fact, I just made that up, but from my experience at least this is what I've noticed. Just like anatomy and perspective, it's a showstopper when it comes to illustrations. When you look at a character and something is anatomically wrong with it, most people will pick it up. While you might not be able to pinpoint exactly what muscle or bone is wrong, you will know something is out of place since you get to see other humans all day long – unless, well, you live in a fantasy world.

Composition on the other hand is a lot more complex and subtle. Everything in the image might be anatomically correct, the colors might be top, the shadows accurate and so on, but you will still feel unease looking at it if the composition is off. This time though, most people will have no clue what's going on or; why they do not love the

image as much as they should. There are a lot of "rules" or guidelines when it comes to composition, and a lot of principles such as shape and proportions, harmony among the elements, the cropping of the picture, color, contrast (light/dark), perspective (when it comes to the focal point this can play a big role) and the orientation of every element to take into consideration.

For this image I chose to focus on color, contrast and the shape and proportions; or the level of detail for every element. Sometimes it's really easy to avoid messing up one of the above principles, such as the orientation. Obviously, I would never have the character where she is, facing the frame of the image instead. It would be the equivalent of having a nose sticking out of the shoulder, anatomically speaking.

COLORS

Starting straight away with colors, rather than grayscale, I wanted this to feel like a speed painting at first – I feel it always adds a bit of energy to

the image (**Fig.01 – 02**). My palette was fairly simple at first: using red as the main color for the focal point, pretty much all the other colors were opposites on the chromatic circle, meaning colors such as blues and greens for the background so as not to attract the eye too much, and vivid saturated colors such as yellows and oranges for the main subject.

Without the parrot or the flower in her hair, my eyes were wandering way too much around the whole image and it didn't feel right. I only added those to help direct the eyes towards the focal point: her face. It's one of the corrections I made almost at the end (**Fig.03a – b**).

CONTRAST

From the very start, I knew I was going to play a lot with the contrast in the scene by simulating walls outside the frame casting shadows on the actual elements in it. The dark area in the bottom left was a result of that, and this is the perfect example of me complicating things for no reason. With the rest of the image fairly bright this area was drawing a lot of

Fig.04

attention away from the girl's face, and as a result the ship in the top right corner had to be brought in to counter this. Same thing with the top left corner: that bit of black rock had me add the rock in the lower right corner to balance the composition (**Fig.04**).

Think of composition as a mathematical equation; if you add something that is not the focal point, the balance is off on one side and you need something equivalent on the other to bring it back.

LEVEL OF DETAIL/SHAPES
Most of the time, tiny details will attract the eye more than plain shapes. I'm not talking about colors of contrast here: if you have less detail in one area, the brain won't put as much effort into understanding it as if it was something very tiny and complex.

A trick to get away with extra details that distract from the main subject is to make all the elements the same color. So, because all her equipment on the deck was really distracting to the eye, and I kind of wanted it still, I just made everything dark and brown (**Fig.05**), as opposed to the region around the face where there are a lot of details going on and a lot of contrast and color variations.

Here again, there is a balance to maintain: if you add too much in one area, like the shipwreck, you need to compensate somehow; hence the subtle yellow color

Fig.05

over it washing off the contrast to make it seem like it's almost just a yellow spot to the eye, telling the brain not to focus too much on it (**Fig.06**).

CONCLUSION
Composition, as I have hopefully demonstrated, can get really complex, really fast. There are a lot of things to keep in mind when starting an image and the extra time spent on composition always pays off. It's like a rollercoaster ride: if your eyes have fun around the image, if they don't get stuck somewhere and always come back to the start (the focal point) – you win!

Fig.06

CHARACTERS

The Beetle Lord
By Nicholas Miles

SOFTWARE USED: Photoshop CS3

INTRODUCTION

Unyielding, relentless, pitiless; he had a heart as hard as the carapace under which it was clad. He had sought dominion over the Insect Dynasty and only the prodigious intervention of the Mantis Queen had thwarted him. In the vacuum of the aftermath lay an uneasy truce. As it had always been, the chosen Beetle Lord existed solely to oppose the Mantis Queen. That was his task, the purpose for which he was created.

WORKFLOW

To choose a Beetle Lord I first needed to explore the variety of Beetle species. This allowed me to get a feel for the key design aesthetics that identified the archetypal beetle, including mandibles, horns, and the shape of the carapace. By keeping elements such as these in mind I hoped the viewer would be able to get a sense of the lineage of the character, even if by completion he were considerably removed from the initial reference.

I started with thumbnails, using a palette knife to keep the designs loose and thus stopping me from "noodling" any one design too much (**Fig.01**). This way I was able to churn through a number of design alternatives very quickly, identifying the traits I wanted to carry through to the next stage and discard those which weren't working.

I knew the Beetle Lord was a character at the pinnacle of his hierarchy, so I wanted to keep the colors rich, evoking the splendor such a position would bestow. With the basic palette in mind I started working directly into color. I added some initial textures to my canvas to create some noise. Psychoigically it can be less intimidating working on a marked canvas as opposed to a white void. Right away I established where my primary light source was coming from. Getting this clear in my mind from the outset made it a lot easier to describe volume, especially on the more complex forms (**Fig.02**).

I kept the brushstrokes broad and bold so as to keep the focus on the larger design features; at this stage the character was still in a state of flux, so there was little point adding detail to features which may be washed

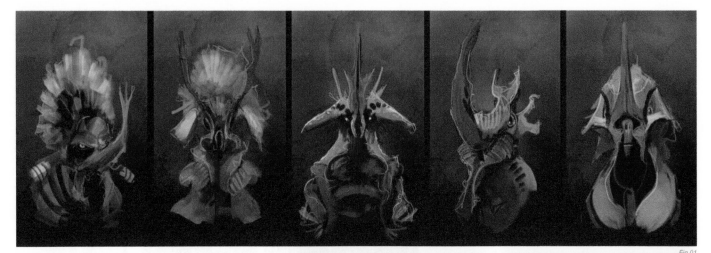

Fig.01

away further into the process. I tried not to zoom in, keeping the whole image in view at this stage, which helped to stop the addition of premature detailing and quickly alerted me if any element was working against another.

All the references I'd acquired furnished me with a strong sense of what I wanted the overall silhouette to look like (**Fig.03**). I further elaborated on this by using simply shaped brushes to both build onto and cut out elements

Fig.04

Fig.02

Fig.03

of this silhouette. I relinquished a certain amount of control by setting the shape brushes to a low level of random scattering. Through the random placement of these brush shapes, and studying the marks they made when they overlaid other forms, I saw new design features I wished to elaborate on that I might otherwise have not considered. Even when I think I have a design tied down, I like to keep an open mind and encourage the process of the well known "happy accident"; this helps to keep the creative process fluid and spontaneous (**Fig.04**).

Custom brushes can be an important part of the creative process. It is, however, all too easy to run amok with them, laying down marks without considering what it is you're trying to achieve. I'd selected roughly a half dozen custom brushes for the Beetle Lord. I chose a number of angular custom brushes which were sympathetic to those aesthetics I'd noted in my references. Some of them can be clearly seen in and around areas such as the eye and horn (**Fig.05**). It is important to consider your choice of brushes – a flowing swirl brush for example would have looked out of place on this character.

A custom brush can be made from just about anything – a montage of photographic elements, brush marks, simple geometric shapes – there is a lot of scope for play. New brushes can even be made from combining other custom brushes, and this is often the quickest way to generate new brushes for experimentation (**Fig.06**).

Once you have your desired custom brush, go to the Edit menu in Photoshop and select the Define Brush Preset option, which will allow you to name and save your brush onto your brush list. Once it's part of your list you can begin to experiment with its presets. These options can be found in the Brushes tab, which if you haven't got open can be found under the Window menu. You can now change properties such as Shape Dynamics, Scattering and a host of others (**Fig.07**).

All these options are there to be explored and adjusted until you get your desired result. The more often you play with these settings the easier it'll become to find

Fig.05

Fig.06

Fig.07

Fig.08

the settings which work for you. Once you have your brush with its adjusted presets it's important to then resave your brush into your brush list so that the new properties are retained.

Describing a variety of surface types on your character will go a long way towards making a rich character design which is more tangible to the viewer. For the most part the Beetle Lord is clad in an armored shell, but in areas which require more articulation, such as the face and neck, the fleshy masses are exposed. I've added bristly hairs between the armor plates – another trait I've noted on many Beetles, which again will help to tie this character in with his chosen source of inspiration (**Fig.08**).

CONCLUSION

Thorough exploration of design routes through thumbnail sketches before committing to a final painting went a long way towards making the Beetle Lord a successful addition to the Insect Dynasty. A good source of reference meant that I had no shortage for sources of inspiration. I focused a lot of my energies on the face, letting the detail fall off away from this focal point so as not to distract the viewer's eye.

Once I have a design and I think I've pushed it as far as I can, I then try to push it further. In retrospect it might have been interesting to push the torso elements, but these are things I can consider for future additions to the Insect Dynasty, of which I'm sure there will be many – perhaps even a successor to the Beetle Lord to once again face down the Mantis Queen?

CHARACTERS

All Images © Nicholas Miles

SEPHIRA
BY NYKOLAI ALEKSANDER

SOFTWARE USED: Photoshop CS

CONCEPT

The idea for the character of Sephira first popped up several years ago, as part of an ongoing story. I hadn't really thought about painting her though until much more recently, when I began painting certain characters from the same story.

I always knew what she would look like, especially since she had to have a strong resemblance to the character of Lucifer (**Fig.01 – 02**). In essence, she had to be like him, both in ethereal beauty and her air of untouchable power, yet still be her own person with her own attitude showing through.

PROCESS

To start off with I made a simple sketch directly in Photoshop, just to capture her looks and get the pose right (**Fig.03**). At this early stage, I never care about

© NYKOLAI ALEKSANDER
Fig.01

© NYKOLAI ALEKSANDER
Fig.02

CHARACTERS

© Nykolai Aleksander

details; it's all about getting the idea down. Once happy with the sketch, I began blocking in the colors with rough brushstrokes, using the default round Paintbrush, and defined her facial features (**Fig.04**). At this point I realized that the light blue background made it all look a bit too pasty, and so I picked some very strong greens and blues to give it a lift (**Fig.05**). After that, more work went into her face and hair to get it to a stage where I could fully concentrate on added details (**Fig.06**).

With the main part of the portrait done, I felt that something needed to go onto her shoulder to break the "block" of skin up a bit. I figured that she should have a tattoo, but before I settled for the serpent you see in the final image, there was a brief moment where I considered a cartoon bulldog, and with that to completely take another direction, away from Sephira and into "stereotypical pretty girl with hardcore tat" territory. I personally would have found it funny because I saw the irony in it (I never paint those kind of things), but that sort of joke usually backfires, and so I returned to the serpent idea.

Lucifer is generally identified with a dragon, so it seemed logical after all to give Sephira one. However, I didn't want to go down the path of a typical dragon, and decided on a water serpent instead. For starters, it was close enough to a normal dragon to be linked with

Fig.03

Fig.04

Fig.06

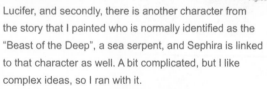

Fig.05

Lucifer, and secondly, there is another character from the story that I painted who is normally identified as the "Beast of the Deep", a sea serpent, and Sephira is linked to that character as well. A bit complicated, but I like complex ideas, so I ran with it.

The general look of the dragon was taken from a design I had come up with a good six years ago, based on Lucifer's appearance. I simply refined it a little, and adapted it to being a water serpent (**Fig.07**). Once the line art was cleaned up (**Fig.08**), I could start thinking about applying color.

CHARACTERS

I wanted the tattoo to look real, part of her skin rather than painted onto her skin. I had never done any colored tattoos before in my work, so trying to figure out how to do this best was a nice little challenge. I wanted the tattoo to reflect the background – it also ties everything nicely together – so I picked one of the shades from the background, added a new layer beneath the line art, and filled in the entire tattoo. No opacity, just plain block color (**Fig.09**). The reason for this is quite simple: once I had the block of color in the shape of the tattoo, I could lock the layer's transparent pixels so I wouldn't need to worry about painting over the edges while detailing the tattoo. It made everything a whole lot easier, even when it was just basic shading (**Fig.10**).

At this point, the tattoo looked very flat and far too dark, and definitely not part of the skin. However, once the layer was set to Overlay, all that changed: it looked way too light, to a point where it was hardly visible. An adjustment of the Levels and Variations helped, and duplicating the layer and setting it to Soft Light added

Fig.07

Fig.08

Fig.09

Fig.10

Fig.11

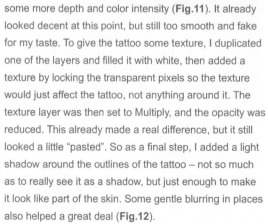

Fig.12

some more depth and color intensity (**Fig.11**). It already looked decent at this point, but still too smooth and fake for my taste. To give the tattoo some texture, I duplicated one of the layers and filled it with white, then added a texture by locking the transparent pixels so the texture would just affect the tattoo, not anything around it. The texture layer was then set to Multiply, and the opacity was reduced. This already made a real difference, but it still looked a little "pasted". So as a final step, I added a light shadow around the outlines of the tattoo – not so much as to really see it as a shadow, but just enough to make it look like part of the skin. Some gentle blurring in places also helped a great deal (**Fig.12**).

With the tattoo done, I suddenly felt that it had taken over the painting, and so I needed to add something that would counterbalance the dragon and pull the girl's face back into focus. Also, there was just too much blue and green in the picture; it needed something to counteract that. I tested it by tentatively adding a red-orange headband (**Fig.13**) matching the serpent's tongue, and liked it so much that I changed the composition. It worked rather well in horizontal orientation, as it let the viewer's eye wander from the flowing scarf over the tattoo and hair to the face: a great example of the Fibonacci Spiral at work (**Fig.14**).

The final steps were refining the scarf and adding the brocade, re-painting the hair and adding texture to her skin – something I love doing, because I can go crazy

Fig.14

Fig.15

Fig.13

with speckled and texture brushes (**Fig.15**)! As a last step, I adjusted the Levels and colors a little, just to really "pop" the greens and reds.

CONCLUSION

All in all I am rather happy with the result, as I believe I succeeded in not only making her look like Lucifer, but also in giving her her own personality. I'm particularly fond of the tattoo now, even though at first I had my doubts about getting it right.

Something I'd do differently – and usually do differently – is the composition of it all. Changing things around halfway through the process can be very annoying and painstaking, and I certainly don't recommend it unless it is really necessary.

The most exhausting part was the hair, without question, mainly because I had to repaint it, and do so within a given time limit. A few people have commented on the way it flows, that it's impossible, and yes, it is quite impossible unless you're standing in the center of a whirlwind or happen to be a non-human entity with supernatural powers, like … Sephira!

© Nykolai Aleksander

© Otherworld

© Otherworld

© Nykolai Aleksander

CHARACTERS

MANOLIA
BY SEBASTIEN HAURE (STUZZI)

SOFTWARE USED: Maya, ZBrush, Mental Ray, RenderMan, Shave&Haircut, Photoshop, BodyPaint and Fusion

INTRODUCTION

In my opinion, it's important for CG art to stay close to other art forms, like photography and painting. With that in mind, I tried to break through the sanitized feel of 3D with this piece with an approach that was perhaps a bit risky, as I tried to tell a story through only a few elements. The main idea was to say more with less.

I wanted to keep interpretation open so that every one of us can have our own take on the image. The ribbon around her face adds a sense of movement to the image as I think it's important that not everything seems fixed, even in a still image. As the image was always intended to be universal the choice of the character's Eurasian features was sensible, and I opted for a black and white intensity for a more dramatic, perhaps even nostalgic feel.

THE CHALLENGE

Artistically, as well as technically, I believe it's important to strive for creativity and to take risks. I've always been fascinated by life captured through the camera lens and intrigued by the practice of trying to create a composition similar to one simulated in a photographic studio. The approach is different, but equally attractive. With CG, we are in sole command and decide every detail before the final touches. In technical terms, we can also push our limits. With this kind of close-up shot, the slightest error will be noticed and can ruin the entire image. We all have a well-trained eye; it requires a lot of patience to fine-tune each detail and a lot of courage to use unusual features or light sources, and to choose non-conformist methods for rendering or compositing. This illustration has been my first step towards a move into photography.

INSPIRATION

I know some very talented photographers and was immediately captivated by their techniques and artistic sensibilities. As I wanted to get closer to their world, I naturally aimed to achieve such a distinctive style in my 3D render. A photographer friend of mine explained to me the rules and directions to follow for such an artistic challenge as this.

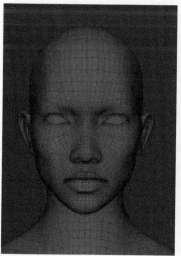

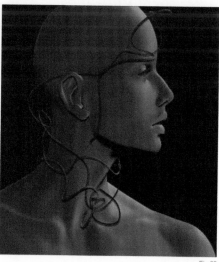

Fig.01

Fig.02

I have had lots of influences, but to name a few I really
like the style of Mathieu Mai and Maurizio Melozzi.
Generally speaking, I often find inspiration in female
glamour models and I rarely find inspiration in 3D artists'
work. The advent of 3D sculpting packages has, I
believe, standardized the type of creations. Over-detailed
creatures flood the galleries. It's a good exercise in
patience or training the eye, but I think we should go back
to less detailed visuals, as details tend to take attention
away from the main image. I'm much more fascinated by
a simple but full-of-life model, than a polished but lifeless
model.

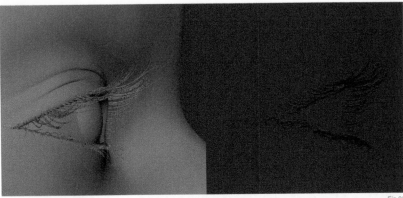

Fig.03

MODELING THE FACE

For this step I mainly used Maya, and then ZBrush for
touch-ups. I started from an existing base mesh of my
own creation, taken from another work-in-progress
(**Fig.01**). I always aim to keep nice topology, unless
the situation calls for otherwise. With this model, some
edges were pinched; I used them as a reference to
stress certain areas and to avoid subdividing too much in
ZBrush.

I always try to keep optimisation techniques in mind in
order to ease the next steps of the creation process
by limiting resources. I don't think the polygon count
increases the refinement of a model; it has more to
do with being accurate with features and volumes. A
realistic female head should not, in theory, exceed 300K
polygons.

I tried to stay subtle and not add too much detail to the
model. That would have, I think, confused the viewer
and harmed the natural feel and realism of the model.
Perceiving material and weight is essential. Areas with
bones or cartilage tend to be firm, whereas fleshy spots

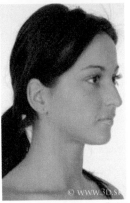

Fig.04a

Fig.04b

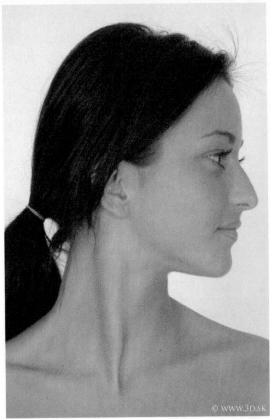

Fig.04c

have a rougher surface. Here is the displacement map
(**Fig.02**); I'm pleased with its definition and its latex feel,
which looks like a special effect prosthetic. The curvature
of the nose and the eyes suggest a Eurasian type, and
the luscious lips hopefully add a glamorous slant to the
image. I opened the mouth in a controlled way to give a
subtle frailty of the neck that occupies a large part of the
image. A sphere was sometimes positioned to make sure
the shape of the eyelid was correct.

EYELASHES

I took advantage of the precision and dynamic properties
of NURBS to draw the eyebrows. The eyelashes'
geometry was extruded along the path represented by
the curve. To make things even easier, I wrote a script
to automate the process and keep the history, to gain

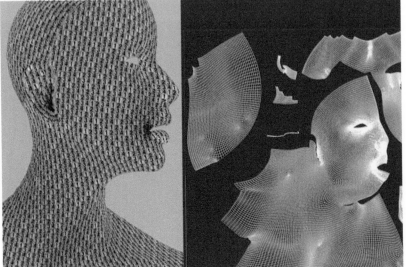

Fig.05

CHARACTERS

flexibility. I can come back and adjust this at any time during the workflow. Finally, I made sure to join the tip of the eyelids and give them random shapes to avoid that 3D feeling of perfection (**Fig.03**).

TEXTURING & HAIR
Having a lot of references for this fundamental step was vital to me; there are plenty of online stock resource sites with high definition photos, such as these from 3d.sk which were particularly useful (**Fig.04a – c**). It's important that light sources are homogenous in all directions, and the main task with this image was toning down the shadows created by the interaction of the light with the irregularities of the surface. I knew the final render would be black and white so it made it easier to create the diffuse map and the shader. The layout of the

Fig.06

Fig.07

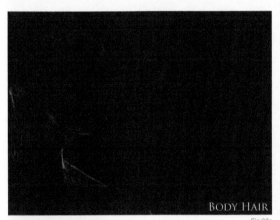
BODY HAIR
Fig.08a

ZDEPTH
Fig.08b

HAIR
Fig.08c

UVs was not that important to me since I was going to work with projections. Only their ratios mattered in this case. It is always important, however, not to use automatic UV unwrapping tools in order to be able to add 2D touch-ups later on (**Fig.05**).

I use a 3D paint tool mainly to make obvious seams disappear and to isolate specific areas, such as the eyes and lips. Doing this helped in creating layers for make-up, spots and blemishes. Skin textures vary a lot from one area to another, of course (**Fig.06**). I then added grayscale textures for the roots of the hair (**Fig.07**).

RENDERING & COMPOSITING
I used Mental Ray for rendering. There was not much light in the scene, so the light directions are obvious. For the kind of mood I was aiming for, two direct lights were

enough. The rectangle area light created accurate, soft shadows, and the shadows were raytraced. I made separate render passes (**Fig.08a – h**) and then desaturated the beauty pass, combining all the passes together in Fusion (**Fig.09**).

CONCLUSION

Photorealism has its own rules. The idea with this piece was to create a character as realistic as possible by

SHADOWS

Fig.08e

FRESNEL

Fig.08f

SPECULAR

Fig.08d

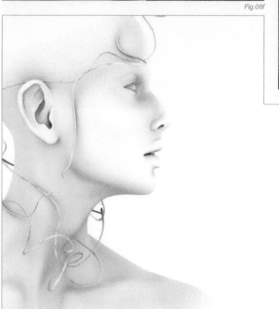

AMBIENT OCCLUSION

Fig.08g

breathing life into her. The main challenge in this kind of work, I believe, is to give a character its own psychology, in order to stray from stereotyped 3D models. I hope I have managed to confuse viewers who may be wondering whether this is a real photo or not, and I also hope to stand out in the 3D landscape which, in my opinion, currently consists of too many recurrent styles. Artists are very talented and I am often amazed by their creations, but I'd like to see even more inventive works in the future. This character corresponds to a kind of ideal but has faults that make her charming. When I was working on the scene's composition I tried to think as a photographer and leave aside the technical aspects of 3D, as they sometimes force us to cheat on or quit a project. I hope I made mine believable in accordance with the style constraints that I chose to work with.

It's difficult to say whether I achieved my original aims with this piece. I hope so, at least. I don't think I can objectively criticise what I do, but from what I have heard so far people seem to appreciate the image and often ask me if it's a photo or a camera mapping. If there are so many questions about it, I guess we can safely assume that the goal was reached. With this in mind the experience has therefore been very positive, and is now a source of motivation for continuing in this direction.

BEAUTY

Fig.08h

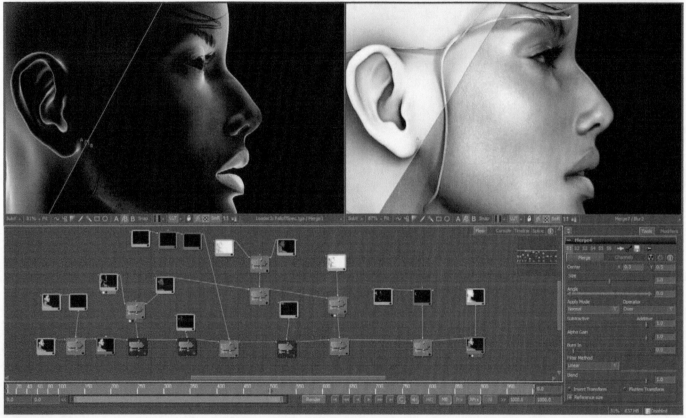

Fig.09

ARTIST PORTFOLIO

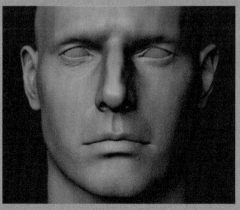

ALL IMAGES © STUZZI

ONLY A WAR MAKES REAL MONSTERS

BY TOMÁŠ MÜLLER

SOFTWARE USED: 3d Studio Max, V-Ray and Photoshop CS3

INTRODUCTION

It has been a while since I started working on this image; to finish it completely took me almost three years, because of other projects and absence of free time. The idea of this work occurred to me when I was browsing through the various CG websites and noticed the large number of monster/creature renders with almost the same composition and content. Later on, I started thinking about making a generic type of creature with a scene and content which makes it look like an artwork that is pointing towards this situation in the CG industry. I also wanted it to carry a tone of self parody. It was a very thin line to work with and it has been quite hard to make the image "speak" properly for itself and to keep it from falling visually into a patronizing or "kitsch" statement within the CG industry.

Fig.01

CONCEPT

Throughout the working process I made lots of changes – on almost everything – to obtain an image that didn't look too funny or even too serious. I started by searching for photographic references of World War II uniforms of all kinds, because I didn't want to use just one kind of uniform as a reference. This led to the final uniform design being a mixture between German SS and Soviet officer uniforms, with some details from the US ones mixed in as well.

After gathering all the main references I made a concept sketch in Photoshop using default brushes (**Fig.01**). As you can see, the sketch is quite different from the final image, including the orientation, design and background content. My first idea was a widescreen illustration with a number of cannons in the background, but I decided to change some of the content to avoid the image looking too illustrative and one-dimensional.

MODELING

For the modeling of the character I created simple base meshes in 3d Studio Max which fitted together the basic shapes of the final model. The base meshes of the figure, and also the background modeling, were done using Editable Polys. The rest of the work, detailing and model changes were done in ZBrush, which is usually my main modeling tool for organic objects (**Fig.02**).

Fig.02

Unwrapping and all UV-map corrections were done in 3d Studio Max. I arranged separate parts of the uniform into SubTools in ZBrush. I wanted to be able to detail and change every part separately, and achieve a good level of detail on each and every one of them. For instance, I separated the base uniform shape, armlet, buttons, button holes, facings, medals, pockets, hat parts, the figure's face and eyes (outer eyeballs and inner ones were made to achieve a feeling of depth inside the eyes) and so on. When the modeling was finished I decreased the subdivision levels in ZBrush to values which still contained the good amount of detail needed for the base models, which were later displaced and textured.

TEXTURING

The texturing for this project was a mixture of basic texture shapes created in ZBrush by poly painting, cavity maps (also from ZBrush), and textures painted in Photoshop. The face diffuse map was made by painting in Photoshop with an additional ZBrush cavity map and a displace map with CCA 20% opacity (**Fig.03**). Other maps were bump (tiling noise procedural map), scatter depth/color (**Fig.04**), a map for the amount of reflection and glossiness (**Fig.05**), and a displace map from ZBrush (**Fig.06**). The textures on the uniform were mostly smaller and tiled, such as the fabric texture (**Fig.07**) and scratched metal parts (**Fig.08**); these were textures from cgtextures.com which were later cropped, overpainted and blended to suit my needs. I also handpainted some textures myself, such as the armlet texture which was painted in Photoshop (**Fig.09**). Almost all of the diffuse textures for the uniform were used also as bump maps (with some image curve tweaks done in 3d Studio Max)

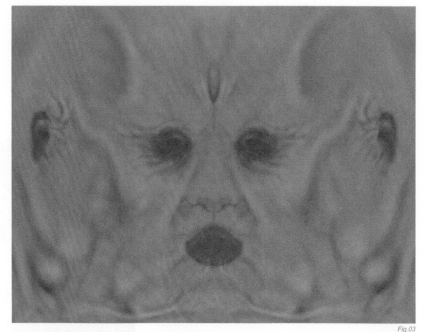

Fig.03

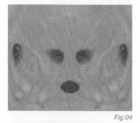

Fig.04

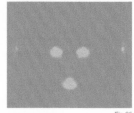

Fig.05

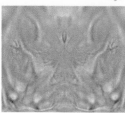

Fig.06

Fig.07

Fig.08

Fig.09

to save system memory for more important things, such as the face textures and more detailed models (this was also the case of the reflection maps and scatter maps for the face).

LIGHTING & RENDERING

The scene was rendered in V-Ray using one warm colored directional light, one blue Omni light placed behind the figure as a backlight, and a small amount of HDRI lighting. I used also Global Illumination to increase the accuracy of the lighting. On all models the VRayMtl shader was used.

The final rendering was done separately from the background as several separate renders mixed together later in post-production in Photoshop. For example, there was the raw render (**Fig.10**), Falloff map (**Fig.11**), Ambient Occlusion pass (**Fig.12**), and a raw render of the background (**Fig.13**). The facial hair was made using Hair and Fur in 3d Studio Max. And, of course, alpha maps were also saved for the masking and compositing of the main parts later on in Photoshop.

BACKGROUND

The background was actually created through a series of very simple tasks. The ground was displaced by two mixed procedural maps (noise and cellular). The anti tank barrier includes a simple model of metal barrier crosses and a deformed spline connected to all barriers. One spline was then later scattered as little spikes to make it look like proper barbed wire. I quickly realized that at this stage the background looked a bit flat and needed to have more layers and a better feeling of space. I decided not to render the additional background layers and to leave this improvement for later on in the post-production process.

Fig.11

Fig.10

Fig.12

Fig.13

POST-PRODUCTION

Photoshop CS3 was used for the compositing of all parts. The main task in Photoshop was to increase the atmosphere and create an enigmatic look. As mentioned before about the background, it was improved during post-production by using an alpha map to mask and duplicate background parts, adding a sky and making the whole background scene consistent through some hand painting over the image. I then blended all of the separate render passes to achieve as complex a look as was possible. I also made some color corrections and contrast adjustments – this took place after all parts of the image had been composed together.

CONCLUSION

At the end of this long time of work I was finally satisfied with the resulting image and its atmosphere, and I'm also glad that I convinced myself to finish it after almost a year and a half without even a single touch on it. I just didn't want to see it ending up unfinished and then later deleted. I'm also pleased to have had the opportunity to share this work with you, and I hope you've enjoyed reading about the process of creation.

ARTIST PORTFOLIO

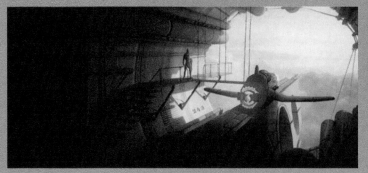

The Smith
By Viktor Titov

SOFTWARE USED: Photoshop

Introduction

Hello, I'm Victor Titov, freelance illustrator and concept artist from Russia. In this article I will try to explain a little about the process and show you some of the techniques used during the creation of *The Smith*. With this image I wished to show a gnome blacksmith working on a new sword; probably deep in thought for a second, or simply observing how heated metal cools down. Aiming for a style similar to a traditional painting, it was interesting for me to create such an unusual atmosphere: pulsing hot air and steam in a blacksmith's workshop.

Sketch & Composition

I usually begin work with a linear sketch or by laying down the general tonal masses at once; with this piece I decided to make a rough linear drawing to start from (**Fig.01**). At this stage it was important to define the

Fig.01

Fig.02

character through its pose and the general silhouette; a blacksmith could be well-fed and muscular, or in contrast he could be rather lean and sinewy. My first problem was in making the blacksmith a gnome, so I had to try and describe his characteristics right from the start in this initial sketch. Because I wanted the work to look almost like a portrait of the character, I didn't choose a dynamic pose – he's simply at work, cooling a blade in a barrel of water.

REFINING THE SKETCH & ADDING A TONAL LAYER

Here I tried to specify the silhouette of my quick sketch, working on a separate layer with thin lines, using a brush similar in feel to a traditional pencil or charcoal (**Fig.02**). The drawing was not too detailed and was kept simple intentionally, as I like to add some subtle changes and details as I work, later on in the process. I simply hid the layer with the initial outline for convenience, and created a new tonal layer, moving it underneath the sketch layer so the sketch was always visible (**Fig.03**). I worked on the tonal layer with a standard round brush with hard edges, sometimes also using textured brushes.

TIME FOR SOME COLOR!

I flooded color onto a new layer in color mode, using a round brush with soft edges (**Fig.04**). The colors were basically all very warm as I was going for an atmosphere of heat, fire and steam, from the fusion of metal in the blacksmith's workshop. I went for different shades of red, orange and yellow. The general color palette which gets laid down here will be enriched by a set of complementary colors during the painting process, just like when painting traditionally.

Fig.03

Fig.04

Fig.05

CREATING A PAINTERLY LOOK/FEELING

I continued applying color using various brushes from my arsenal, working towards creating a living and breathing structure (**Fig.05**). My painting at this stage actually reminded me of a pastel drawing, when the different colors are applied to paper and partially blended, but not blocked in completely, creating a variety of harmonious combinations.

LIGHTING & CONTRAST

I illuminated the character by adding the effect of a bright yellow light behind him, as well as a more obvious saturated red light in front from the red hot metal (**Fig.06**). As there should always be an accent in an image, I gave particular attention to the character's face, studying touches of light on his folds of skin and in his beard.

As a whole, the colors at this stage of the painting process were given more contrast and became much deeper, using different brushes, such as those shown in **Fig.07 – 08**, in order to create a sense of a variety in the textures and keeping a similarity with traditional painting.

CORRECTIONS

Here I started to correct the painting, adding the edge of the barrel and moving and rotating the sword a fraction. I also changed the lighting slightly, creating a deeper darker shade from above the character and strengthening the light coming from below. All this gave additional contrast and separated the figure from the background more strongly (**Fig.09**).

One of the most enjoyable Photoshop tools that I use to create a sense of brushstrokes is the Smudge tool (**Fig.10**). If you want to use this tool properly you should

Fig.06

Fig.07

Fig.08

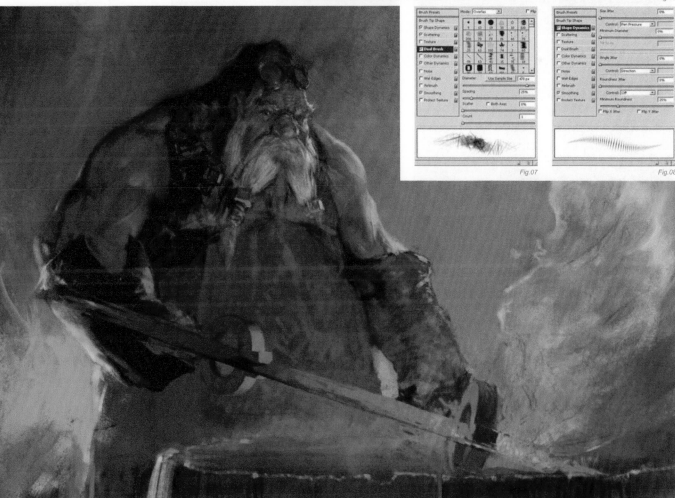

Fig.09

experiment and use it with various brushes, because the brush with the Scattering parameter turned on will give you one effect, and a brush with Texture option applied will give you a totally different result. One of my favorite brushes for using with the Smudge tool is shown in **Fig.11**. It's also possible to use this tool to achieve the mixing of colors similar to traditional media, such as oil or acrylic. You can get the same effects using Painter or ArtRage, but sometimes it's simply more convenient to do everything in one program.

DETAILS & FINISHING TOUCHES

I continued detailing the work, creating layers for more fine details and giving more clarity and completeness to the work, such as the buckle on his clothes, the bright red patches of light catching the folds of his clothes and gloves, the highlights in his eyes, the reflections on the sword, and the screw nuts twisted into his beard.

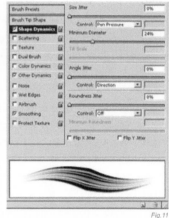

Fig.11

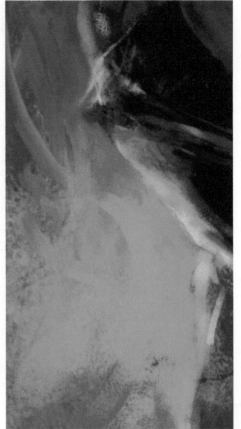

Fig.10

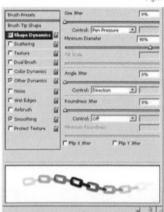

Fig.12

Fig.13a

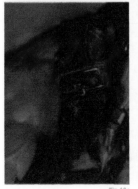

Fig.13c

Fig.13d

Fig.13b

You must never forget the light sources in your illustrations. For example, with *The Smith*, a cold greenish light on the right helped to focus attention on the character's face and arm; the light picks up all those fine details, such as the muscles, veins, skin folds, etc.

Finally, here is another, more cunning use of brushes in Photoshop. If you have a problem drawing repeated details, such as a hanging chain, the glowing windows of a skyscraper, and the rivets on the hull of a spaceship, for example, then try to create yourself a custom brush that will not only simplify your problem, but will also help speed up the entire process. The brush which helped me to create the chains hanging in the background in just in a few minutes can be seen in **Fig.12**. I then simply added highlights to the chain links, painted in some steam from the barrel of water with a soft brush, and added some small spotlights in the background to give more depth to the entire image. As my finishing touch I made some minor color correction, adding warmer red and yellow tones. And I was done (**Fig.13a – d**).

CONCLUSION

I learned so much through the process of painting this image, and more importantly I also had a lot of fun creating it. I really hope you can find something useful from this brief walkthrough and have enjoyed the insight into the creation of *The Smith*.

ON THE PRECIPICE OF THE UNIVERSE
BY ALEXEY KASHPERSKY (RIDDICK)

SOFTWARE USED: ZBrush, 3d Studio Max and Photoshop

INTRODUCTION
The idea for this artwork was born when I was wandering through the open spaces of the internet, and casually stumbled across a very interesting photograph of two girls, taken by Olga Shelegeda (**Fig.01a**). Instinctively, I wanted to work a little on the composition of the photograph, and so, starting by twisting the photograph in Photoshop, I continued to paint over the image in search of my desired composition (**Fig.01b**).

After spending some time considering the concept, I clearly started to envisage the future work. The concept did not raise any complications for me, since right from the outset it was clear to me that most of the work should be in the form of a 3D sculpture; I really wanted to test myself with this work because beforehand I had only ever sculpted figures using traditional clay (**Fig.02**).

First of all, I wanted to make the whole work completely in ZBrush, to study the opportunities of the software in more depth. Eventually I realized that if I wanted to achieve a high quality render it was going to be necessary to export the sculpture into 3d Studio Max to render, because the renderer in ZBrush loses the quality that V-Ray or Mental Ray can achieve, by comparison.

MODELING & COMPOSITING
I began from a low poly model created by Andrey Kravchenko, used purely for the sake of economy of time, which I imported into ZBrush (**Fig.03**). I started with the bottom figure, as this approach seemed the least difficult to me. The first thing that was necessary was to find a pose and the general form of the figure. In ZBrush, this was achieved by using the Transpose tool (unfortunately, using the Transpose tool deformed the figure, but this was easily corrected later on).

I find it is always important to correctly expose the bone structure at this initial sculpting stage. Gradually, after laying down the largest body masses, I could then move onto the smaller items such as the hands and fingers to establish my figure in the desired proportions (**Fig.04 – 05**). It doesn't matter what you create, be it a 3D sculpture or a painting done in Photoshop, it is always necessary to observe and follow a simple rule: to conduct

© SHELEGEDA OLGA
Fig.01a

© ALEXEY KASHPERSKY (RIDDICK)

Fig.01b

Fig.02

Fig.03

Fig.04

Fig.05

Fig.06

your work from the general form to the final details. How much time you spend on the creation of your work is down to you, but your final work should always look fresh and vivid, as though it was created in just half an hour's inspiration

Before starting to transpose the second model, I defined for myself the basic masses and found the center of gravity between the two characters by reverting back to the concept piece. For me, this was a key moment in the creation of such a complex pose (**Fig.06**). And it is on this note that I'd like to mention a mistake that many artists often make during the creation of human or humanoid characters … If figures look unbelievable or fail then the reason is simple: the center of gravity has not been found. It usually passes through the seventh cervical vertebra and falls in a heel bone. In a vertical static pose this rule always works (**Fig.07**).

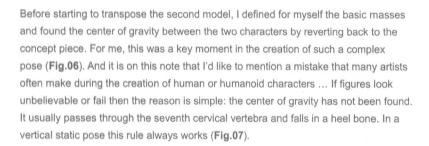

Fig.07

Both figures were posed at this stage, and it was then possible to start adding more detail and combine both of the models together. At this stage there were still rough anatomical mistakes, such as in the thigh areas, their improbable breasts and the pressed down buttocks, and the positions of their heads and necks still left much to be desired. As I was working on the models, I started to consider the plinth upon which these girls would be settled. There were two variants of plinth that I had in mind (**Fig.08 – 09**), but I later returned to the original concept sketch which saw the girls posed on the edge of a rock. Since the beginning I had intended the rock to be more decorative than realistic, and so I needed to create an object that was not just your average rock, but a decorative element of a composition reminiscent of the material.

It was here that I started to think about their hair (**Fig.10**). Another rule that I like to follow when creating my artwork is to try and conduct work that is regular in all areas. This keeps integrity in the work at any stage. You should always conduct work in such

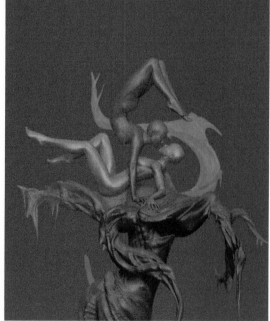

Fig.08

a manner that at any stage it could be taken and put in a frame to hang up in an exhibition.

Once all the details of the composition had been worked out approximately and equally, it was possible for me to have a rest from the work, and so I took some time to step back from it and, after a while, look at the image with a fresh pair of eyes (**Fig.11**). It's always easier to notice any defects or flaws in the image after your eyes and mind have had a break from working on it.

Fig.09

Fig.10

FANTASY

TEXTURES

After correcting some parts of the image that I felt were flawed, I started "painting" my textures, still working in ZBrush, always keeping in mind that the work was intended to be decorative. At this stage I precisely understood that the bottom girl was going to have a lighter toned skin and red hair; the girl on top was going to be somewhat darker (**Fig.12**). After several experiments, I stopped on an almost white color of hair for the young lady on top.

When painting skin I always keep in mind that there is a dark blue color present where the blood vessels are close to the surface. This occurs primarily at the bottoms of the legs, hands and fingers; the skin appears more yellow in places where there is a higher concentration of fatty tissue, such as the hips and breasts. Skin also appears darker in areas where there is more hair growth. To conclude the texturing phase of the artwork in 3D, I decided to add some decorative elements to the girls' faces, hair and legs (**Fig.13**) to enhance the decorative nature of the image.

Fig.11

Fig.12

3D STUDIO MAX & POST-PRODUCTION

With this particular artwork I didn't use any UV unwrapping or anything like that, just ZBrush UV textures. I exported the high-poly models and covered them with the painted textures. I then created three Omni light sources plus HDRI; the two dark blue Omni lights created a nice cold reflection to counterbalance the warm VRay Sun. I then rendered the scene using the V-Ray renderer, and the file was saved as a .TIFF with an alpha channel – I didn't even use any SSS!

Post-production in Photoshop consisted of the adjustment of the brightness and contrast, the addition of some clouds and a background via the alpha channel of the final render, and I also used the Lighting Effects filter and a plug-in called Alien Skin Exposure to finish up work on the image.

CONCLUSION

Any artist should be able to paint a door in their home, but not every house-painter will be able to paint a picture. The same applies here: to be a CG artist it's not enough to know only the programs; it is not enough to have simply the knowledge of techniques; one needs to become an artist. It is an obligation as an artist to study, to feel the art and the melody of each and every line of a drawing, every bend of a sculpture, because there is no such thing as a "make beautiful" button built into your software!

I would say that this particular artwork has become a turning point in my creative search; I have completely refused those devices used in my latest 3D works, and I have started to think in another way…

Fig.13

ARTIST PORTFOLIO

20.000 Miles Lost
By Blaz Porenta

SOFTWARE USED: Photoshop

INTRODUCTION

I simply love working on projects like this one, a challenge run by CGSociety. No tight deadlines, a theme that can be widely interpreted, and a bust of motivation by fellow artists commenting on your work and doing their own. Painting purely for fun and building up your portfolio is one of the most satisfying things an artist can ask for.

WORKFLOW

My working process varies from painting to painting. Sometimes I start from a pencil sketch, other times I begin by mixing brushstrokes and searching for a nice composition that will tell me how to continue. I love experimenting, not knowing what will happen next, so I try many different things and see what works and what doesn't. I just try to keep in mind some basic rules of art theory, which will hopefully make the painting well balanced and easy to read.

Fig.01

In this case, I started by searching for a nice composition, before any story or characters were defined. I knew they would pop up eventually, so I just went with the flow, took some interesting brushes – as scattered and textured as possible – and created a bunch of abstract strokes (**Fig.01**). The first forms started to appear; some like figures, others like objects (a signpost for example), and a story quickly revealed itself in my

Fig.02

Fig.03

head. A fierce army of undead creatures is marching to their final battle, but they get lost on their way ... and where better to put Hell's lost army than into a freezing cold environment? A rough concept is made so I can go on, set an early color scheme, design some of the characters and see how everything works together.

As the canvas size limited me on portraying a really huge army, I expanded it and got a lot of room for more soldiers on the left side, as well as some extra space on the right to show more of the environment

they found themselves in (**Fig.02**). In moments like this you really appreciate working digitally and not being limited to any number of changes. I also established the initial color scheme here in a rather cold blue hue, with some reds here and there to liven the whole image up a bit.

With everything finally being roughly defined (the story, the composition, colors and so on) I switched back to grayscale mode and started adding the first details and designing my various characters (**Fig.03**). I generally

Fig.04

FANTASY

153

Fig.05

switch between color and grayscale mode regularly, always checking if the painting works well both ways and if the depth is still readable. Too often it can happen that detailing with colors will lead into too many tonal variations and the image can become confusing.

Being happy with the amount of detail in grayscale mode, it was time to bring the previously selected colors back (**Fig.04**). This was easily done by dropping some color and overlay mode layers on top of the base image. I find Overlay mode really useful: whilst coloring everything under it, it can also accent some of the highlights and darken the shadows, if needed.

From here on it was mostly painting as I would do with acrylic colors – small brushstrokes to sculpt the characters out of the background, lots of detailing and polishing (**Fig.05**). While in this stage, I am always open to new things that might pop up in my head. So if at

Fig.06

Fig.07

any stage of the process I feel a character doesn't fit in anymore, I delete it and paint another one from scratch, or I change the whole color scheme if the present one starts to get boring (**Fig.06 – 07**).

In the rendering stage I like to make my paintings vivid and "alive", so I try to use saturated colors as much as I can, whilst being careful not to exaggerate and make it look "burnt". To still keep things as real and believable as possible, regardless of the theme I am portraying, I

Fig.08

Fig.09a

Fig.09b

Fig.09c

do a lot of research and gather as many photographic references as I can. In this case, I was checking mostly for colors that snow could reflect, and found everything from blue, pink to orange hues – perfect for this type of illustration! I also prefer to leave lots of unfinished areas and raw brushstrokes in my paintings, especially those areas in the back where shapes are actually just hints of actual elements and left for the viewer's imagination to do the rest. To achieve that look, I use custom brushes (**Fig.08**), some of which are my own, and some I download from various artists' web pages. I would like to give credit here to the artists known as Goro, m@ and Barontieri for their brush packs, which I use most often and throughout all of my works.

At the end of every painting, when the rendering process is sort of finished (**Fig.09a – c**), I start playing with textures and adding some of the last touches. For textures I often use different photos of rust and dirt, sometimes scanned acrylic brushstrokes, and overlay them on the painting. Every texture I place in is carefully chosen and refined on parts that don't enrich the basic image.

Lately I've also experimented a lot with Photoshop's Bas Relief filter, which adds some sort of depth to brushstrokes (**Fig.10**). This filter, as well as texture layering, mustn't be overused, as it easily becomes cheesy if visible too much or shown in the wrong places.

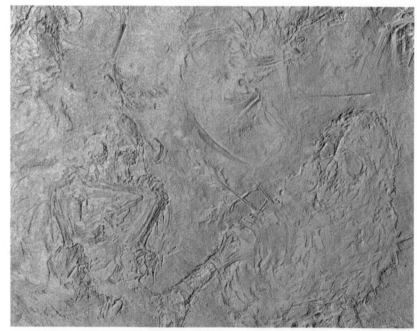
Fig.10

Fig.11a

Fig.11b

After texturing, it was time for those final touches, slight color corrections and last moment details, such as adding mist, dust particles and snowflakes – something which will tie the whole piece together and make it work as a whole, as well making it more believable (**Fig.11a – b**).

CONCLUSION

I wish my tight schedule would allow me to spend more time working on pieces like this one; to just kick back and relax, paint without any stress of being late for deadlines or changing everything just because a client isn't a big fan of the color blue. But at least this way I can appreciate those rare moments even more.

© KEKAI KOTAKI

WARBAND
BY KEKAI KOTAKI

SOFTWARE USED: Photoshop CS2

INTRODUCTION

I started *Warband* as a piece to create in my free time. Doing concept work professionally is fun, but I enjoy painting on my own as well. The original idea for this piece came up while I was reading a fantasy novel. The basic premise was a fantasy creature waging war on mankind. One thing that really stuck out for me was that after these creatures plundered the town, the survivors heard the creatures celebrating and thought that their singing was beautiful. Inspired, an image of a prowling herd of fantasy creatures became the foundation for this piece.

Fig.01

GETTING STARTED

When starting an image I start very loosely, nothing much more than textures and brushstrokes (**Fig.01**), but there are some things that I plan on having beforehand. I like to have a main focal point, which in this case is the leader of the pack of creatures. So blocking him out was one of the first things that I did (**Fig.02**). I worked loosely on this piece, since I was creating it in my free time and didn't have any particular design criteria I had to meet.

Fig.02

Fig.03

As you can see, I work in a very monochromatic fashion. Most of these browns and grays come from me layering different textures whilst I paint, as shown previously in **Fig.01**. I like to keep my mind focused on designing the main points, which at this stage was the leading character of the image. Hints of other figures also started to appear here since I had a fairly strong sense of what I wanted from the main character (**Fig.03**). The composition of the overall piece was also being revealed to me at this stage, with the leader of the group surrounded by his many followers.

PAINTING…

With a strong sense of what I wanted now, I began rendering the main character (**Fig.04**). The helmet was loosely based on a deer's skull. I tried to get an antler vibe from the horns on his helmet, too. I started rendering the pieces of the armor and weaponry, picking a mace as his weapon of choice as it just seemed brutal enough for this particular piece. I also used a photograph to help

Fig.04

me with the design on his clothing, still not working on the other characters too much at this stage – just moving pixels around, trying to get a very loose idea of what I wanted to do with them. I like to use the Soft Light layer in Photoshop; this is how I leak colors into a piece, like the yellows shown in **Fig.04**.

Liking what I'd done with the main character for now, I got started on the rest of the pack. Some loose line drawings gave me a sense of the flow of the piece (**Fig.05**), and this was followed by me fleshing out the line work (**Fig.06**). Loosely blocking out figures is something I love to do; it's quick and messy. From here I spent some time trying to pull out the new figures in the painting.

…MORE PAINTING

One thing I haven't talked about yet is how many times I like to flip my canvas whilst I work. It's a common trick many artists use in order to check whether their composition is working out or not. I like to do this so much that I have made a shortcut for it in Photoshop. Something to think about is making your workspace tailored to you – you will use it a lot, so make it as easy and comfortable to use as possible.

I used another Soft Light layer here to give the entire piece a warmer feel (**Fig.07**), and I was getting a better idea of what the side characters were going to look like. From here I started detailing out the armor and such, also using some fur references to help me out with the wolves

Fig.05

Fig.06

as they were lacking a certain "punch" to them. I decided to put stripes on them to give them a different vibe to your regular wolves (**Fig.08a**), but then when I looked at the whole image here I realized that certain elements of the design had started to get lost in the process, so I needed to take care of that.

Wrapping Things Up

One thing I try to keep in mind when I'm working on a piece is that, even though many things are happening, I must try to keep track of everything. When I was rendering out one of the wolves, I was – at the same time – slowly adding more armor detail to the goblin in the background (see **Fig.08b**). This was also the point when I started to organize the "mess" I had created for myself – separating out elements and giving more detail to others.

This was the home stretch of the image now. The mace got a little lost, so putting a strong highlight on it helped to bring it out a bit. I also separated the different elements out further by using some glow and haze. Desaturating the different pieces of armor also helped to break them up a little more. Some more small details, like spears,

Fig.07

Fig.08a

Fig.08b

Fig.09

were added to the piece for more visual information, and one final trick I used was the Elliptical Marquee tool, which I used to make a circle selection on a Soft Light layer and paint in the white circles over the three characters. I then used this to frame what I thought were the three prominent figures (**Fig.09**).

Finally

I had fun doing this piece and I got to practice my craft. I was able to do something that I wanted to do, and as an artist I can't really ask for anymore than that. Am I satisfied? No, of course not! As an artist I feel I can always do better. Or that I should do better. One thing that I wish I could go back and change is the beauty of the piece – I'd love to make the image more beautiful. I believe I got the war part right, but I would have loved to be able to achieve a "beautiful singing" element in the work, too, like what I felt from my original inspiration … but I guess that would require a different piece altogether. Maybe next time!

MAKE ME PROUD...
BY MAREK OKOŃ

SOFTWARE USED: Photoshop CS2

INTRODUCTION

Make me proud... was an image created for one of *ImagineFX* magazine's "Workshops" articles. The initial idea behind the creation of this image was to study light and shadow in a full sunlit environment, and to consider all of the characteristics and traps of such a scene that a painter would undoubtedly face when tackling bright sunlight.

CONCEPT

Some of you may have seen my work already and will know that I like to add extra elements of story to my images, to try and keep the viewer's attention for that extra minute. The best location for the study of sunlight is of course the desert, and so I chose to paint a rocky desert valley within a fantasy world, featuring the huge artifacts left behind by some technologically advanced species. In the scene we witness dragons being used as a heavy duty work force, a group of dragon tamers all trying to manage a dragon on the loose, and on a more nostalgic note we also see a father in the foreground leading his son for his first day as a dragon tamer. Like father, like son.

SKETCHES

After the idea was formed I painted a few quick sketches, just to pick the best composition for my scene. I usually find that one of my doodles is close enough in order for me to proceed with the painting (**Fig.01**). At this stage,

Fig.01

Fig.02

the sketch work was fast and loose – just a few lines and values. I wanted to be able to change it without losing too much work.

LIGHT CONSIDERATION

Even before I laid my first brushstroke on this painting, I had to secure in my mind what was going to be important in a sunlight environment. First of all, the global light source is the sun; it's very strong and direct, with a light yellow (or orange if you're working on a sunset/sunrise scene) hue. It also casts very sharp shadows that will nicely sculpt the form of the subject you are painting. The second global light source is of course the blue sky. This light is almost invisible in direct sunlight, but it's revealed

Fig.03

in the shadows that are created by the sun. The sky is a dome light which is scattered, because we are basically surrounded by it, mainly from the top and sometimes from the sides; it creates shadows that are soft, blurry and fade quickly, due to the Omni-directional nature of the sky light.

On top of this theory I also had to calculate the indirect light sources created by the sunlight. In full sunlight practically everything is bouncing some of the light back, and it can be quite difficult to keep track of it. This is what makes painting things in full sunlight a much tougher experience: the multiple light sources.

LIGHT SETUP

So after analyzing the behavior of sunlight, which after some time comes to you so naturally that you don't even have to think about it, I made my first color sketch (**Fig.02**).

Fig.05

Fig.06

The colors were slightly exaggerated, and I did this just to see how my lighting setup was working more clearly.

The father and son characters are standing in the sun's shadow, but they are still partially illuminated by the sky light (demonstrated by the blue arrows in **Fig.03**). This is why they have a bluish cast with soft shadows all around them. The dragon on the other hand is illuminated directly by the sun (demonstrated by the white arrows); he has nice sharp shadows cast by his muscles, neck and wings – notice that his left and bottom sides are completely shielded from the sun. It's in the sun's shadow that other lights come to life! Almost every shadow on the dragon's body has a bluish hue from the sky light, although there are places that this sky light won't reach at all, such as under the wings or on the dragon's tummy. And those are also places where some bounced light (demonstrated by the red arrows) appears – a warm yellow/orange light bounced from the sand and rocks. The same thing happens when it comes to the bottom of the cliff and the overhang. The only difference is that inside the overhang we have no trace of any blue sky light, because it's completely cut off from it – and thus dark.

PAINTING

With the basic lighting setup down, I moved on to the shape blocking and object rendering work, remembering not to go into the details too soon and to develop the image equally (**Fig.04**) (otherwise I would have had to later rework areas that didn't gel well with one another). In these early stages I was using a basic round brush to quickly define the shape and volume of the objects (**Fig.05**). From time to time I also used a flat round brush to make nice clean lines on the ground and rocks. Flipping the image horizontally several times also helped keep things looking fresh in my mind; this technique helps to catch most of the mistakes early on.

I continued adding more and more elements from my initial concepts, applying the same light rules previously mentioned to each new addition to the scene (**Fig.06**), working my way through the image from the background to foreground, pass after pass, adding more detail, textures and objects (**Fig.07**). Once I was happy with the results I applied some atmospheric effects – dust, halos, aerial perspective (**Fig.08**). And finally, I balanced the whole image with a few adjustment layers with masks for different planes and elements in the picture (**Fig.09**).

CONCLUSION

Well that's pretty much it; everything else comes down to technicalities, which I think are less important than

Fig.07

the knowledge and understanding of the basic principles behind any painting. When you understand the universal rules it doesn't matter what program or textures or brushes you are using.

Working on this image allowed me the time to understand more of the nuances and behavior of light under different environmental conditions, and in the end I was also quite satisfied that I had managed to successfully combine a purely technical exercise with some deeper story telling.

Fig.08

Fig.09

© Marek Okoń | Client: Fabryka Słów

© Marek Okoń | Client: Fabryka Słów

© ImagineFX Magazine

© Marek Okoń | Client: Fabryka Słów

© ImagineFX Magazine

© Roberto Fernández Castro

THE BACK-ALLEY
BY ROBERTO F · CASTRO

SOFTWARE USED: Photoshop CS3

INTRODUCTION

The intention with my paintings is always to create a good concept. In this picture I was trying to evoke an atmosphere that could transport the observer to a different place and age. The idea was to create a narrow location where the architecture was the unique element that defined the space. I did some architectural sketches to find a perfect balance between fantasy and medieval styles (**Fig.01a – b**). These drawings were helpful to get a clear concept about the architectural style, but the idea of *The Back-Alley* was more the "space" itself. Right from the beginning, the intention was to give the same importance to the architecture as well as the space.

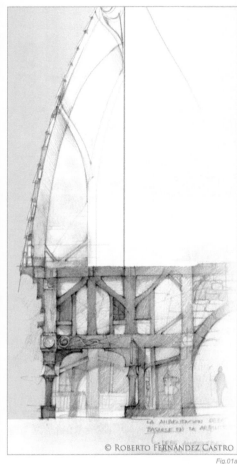

© Roberto Fernández Castro

Fig.01a

Fig.01b

Drawing Technique

Regarding my painting technique, I have created around twenty brushes that I use in my work. This image was one of the first I did with a graphic tablet, so I didn't use strange or specific brush designs. The tool I use most of the time is a simple brush with pressure opacity and a light irregular texture that avoids a sharp artificial finish. With this picture I preferred using vertical flattened shapes to simulate a perspective effect, and the vertical lines were painted thinner than the horizontal ones (**Fig.02**).

I start my drawings with a medium-sized document that I increase as the image progresses. In terms of workflow, I try not to focus on only one area of the piece but instead work on maintaining the same amount of detail throughout. I put down loose forms of color which I gradually add detail to as I advance through the painting. I've selected four images to illustrate this working process for this particular image (**Fig.3a – d**).

I'm not going to center my explanation on my drawing technique as it's not an important element in the scene. This image has more important things to discuss, so I'm going to focus the rest of my article on composition, color and lighting concepts.

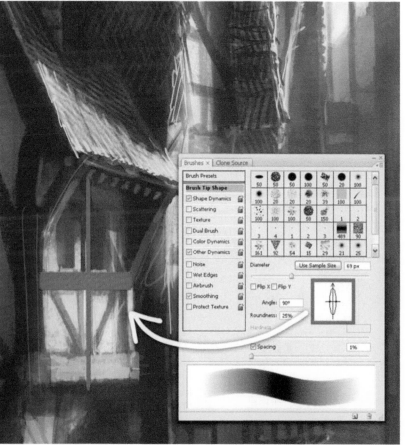

Fig.02

COMPOSITION

I think too many Photoshop layers make the drawing process difficult, giving an artificial appearance to the painting. In this scene I worked with three main layers (**Fig.04**): the building close-up on the right (red), the medium distanced houses that border the alley (blue) and the background with buildings in the distance (yellow). It was a good decision to create the layers depending on the depth in the scene because I could easily control the color saturation and brightness of each layer to simulate the effect of distance.

Fig.03a

Fig.03b

Fig.03c

Fig.03d

Fig.04

I used the color and composition to keep a general vision of the image, and I painted the entire image with a small range of colors (**Fig.05**). The afternoon sunlight coats the building surfaces with reddish and golden tones. The horizon line is located approximately in the lower third of the height of the buildings (that is, if the observer is

on the balcony) (**Fig.06**). This perspective allowed me
to contemplate all the buildings from one angle without
a strange or forced perspective. The image also has
a vertical composition, and the pointed and stylized
architecture is over-sized compared with the people
walking on the street (their equivalent to ten floored
structures), but this isn't a problem – the scene evokes
an unreal and oneiric feel.

LIGHT & SHADOW

One thing that I find incredibly important in this kind
of semi-realistic scene is the treatment of light. I like
to emphasize light in my pictures. I think that creating
lighting effects to give the scene a dramatic and magical
appearance is essential in order to reach a satisfactory
result. In the dark alley the light passes through the
buildings to illuminate the space. It's a great moment! In
some way, the observer can guess the time of the day,
and with this theatrical light I am directing the viewer
where I want him to look.

I created the effect with a layer set in Overlay blending
mode (**Fig.07**). I used a pale yellow to lighten the building
surface; the difference can be noted (**Fig.08a – b**). The
shadowed zones acquire an orange brightness that
simulates the sun's reflection. It's useful to include other
layers and brushes with different mix types, such as

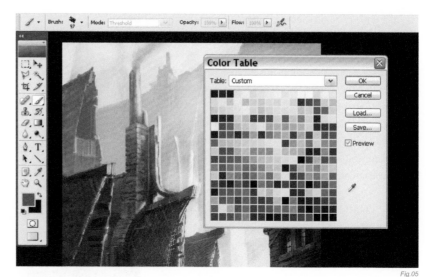

Fig.05

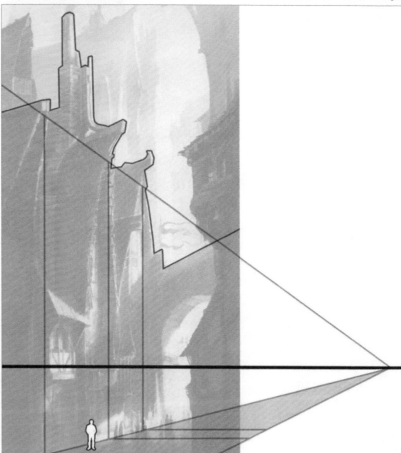

Fig.06

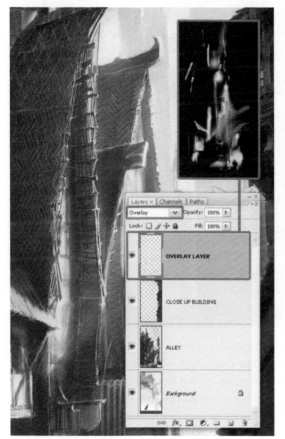

Fig.07

Overlay or Multiply blending modes, which in turn provide good lighting and shading
effects without sacrificing any of the details of the drawing.

This image has harsh lighting conditions, which I've represented with two plain colors
(**Fig.09**). It's very important to understand how light and shadow work. In a more
detailed view the differences are evident. The direct light reveals the sharpened
contour of the objects and the brushstrokes are better defined (**Fig.10**); on the other
hand, the darker areas are roughly painted. As hard to believe as it may seem, this
technique is helpful in order to create a realistic ambience. Unconsciously, in the real
world, the observer usually gives more importance to the illuminated areas of objects,

and the decision to give more detail to these areas is an important and difficult task in any painting.

In *The Back-Alley* many areas are low in detail. I think that an artwork is finished when the artist reaches the objectives he has in mind, and this statement is one of the key points of any artistic work. Some illustrations do not need a high level of detail. In many cases success doesn't depend on the hours of work detailing parts of the scene without any aesthetic criterion!

CONCLUSION

In the end, I reached my goal. The final result is interesting. The challenge was to define a space with a

Fig.08a

Fig.08b

Fig.09

Fig.10

fantasy style building. As an architect, I think that the light is the essence of the architecture. The empty space and the solid elements have the same importance. However, the true protagonist is the alley itself, not the architecture. I don't think this image has a refined style, but the painting technique doesn't matter – a strong idea is an essential key to the success of an image.

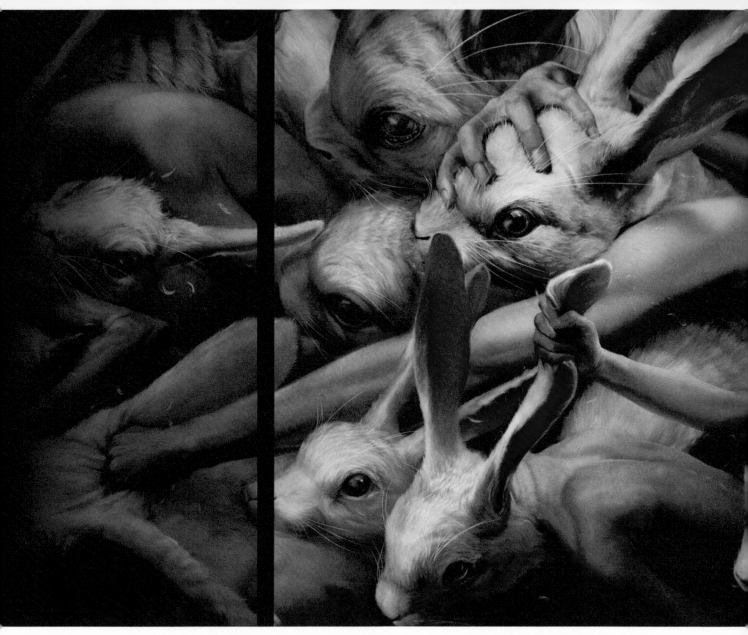

GO FORWARD AND FORWARD
BY RYOHEI HASE

SOFTWARE USED: Photoshop CS3

INTRODUCTION

When creating illustrations I always try to depict anxious feelings, as well as show the vanity of human nature. I often get inspiration from the people around me; they could be my friends, my girlfriend, or a complete stranger – everyone has something to inspire me, just in varying degrees. I came up with the idea of *Go forward and forward* when I was walking through the crowds in Tokyo. People were walking forward and forward without any expression, without looking back. I could feel the strength of the people through their eyes, but at the same time the whole scene made me feel quite sad (as well as a little scared).

I tend to use animals' faces or other objects, rather than human faces, in order to show expressions and feelings. For example, I personally see a monster when I watch a person who is raging with anger – that kind of thing. Sensuously, I mean. To make my illustrations interesting and impressive, this technique of substituting humans with

© RYOHEI HASE

Fig.01

FANTASY

© RYOHEI HASE

animals can often be very effective, and for this particular artwork the blank faces of rabbits were a perfect subject for my concept.

In terms of the composition, by connecting the beginning to the end and the end to the beginning, I realized that I could create a strong feeling of repetition – almost like an endless journey of human life. For me, creating interesting ideas is the most important part of my art production.

© RYOHEI HASE

Fig.02

Fig.03

No matter how beautifully I paint, nothing will work out without a good idea behind it!

For this piece I didn't make any drafts of the scene because I had a perfect vision in mind for how it would look, but I did paint a rabbit using watercolors – just for practice (**Fig.01**). I usually paint digitally, but sometimes I also like to paint with traditional tools in order to not forget the sense of traditional painting (**Fig.02**). I would say that if you're keen to improve your digital painting skills, then practicing with traditional material is the quickest way to success.

WORKFLOW

I used Photoshop as my painting tool to create this image. I first of all sketched the overall image with a brush, which was similar in technique to drawing on paper – no special techniques. The composition was a very important part of this image so I had to pay attention to this. To give the image impact I mixed various poses and sizes of the characters to avoid any monotony in the composition. Also, in my case, I tend to lose the composition and my light values when working with color, so I started painting this image with gray only, to help avoid this situation (**Fig.03**).

At this point, I used the offset filter to make the image "repeatable"; basically, I moved the image and connected the edges by adding some parts. I then moved the image back to its original position. After continuing work on the image to some extent, I then colored the image with a gradient map (**Fig.04**) – yellow was used for the highlights and purple for the darker shade (**Fig.05**).

By now, it was ready to paint in the detail. By paying attention to how rabbits' coats of fur grow, and aiming not to lose the overall appearance of solidity, I carefully painted in the detail (**Fig.06**), starting by detailing the rough hair with a round brush (**Fig.07** – Step 1). I then used the smudge tool to blend the rabbits' fur at the roots (**Fig.07** – Step 2) and painted in the fine hairs, again blending them with the smudge tool. I also created a custom brush to paint the fur in order to make the

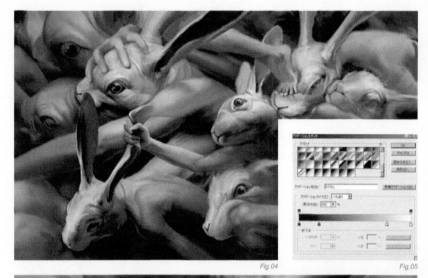

Fig.04   Fig.05

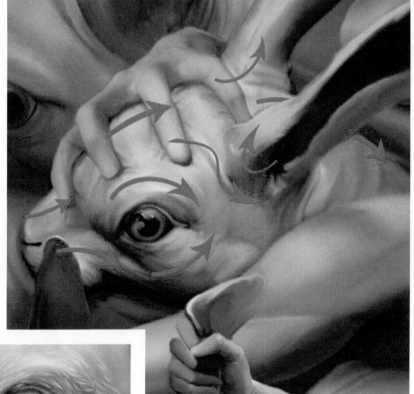

Fig.06

process much easier, as it was repeated many times and took a long time to complete (**Fig.07** – Step 3). Finally, I emphasized the contrast using the burn and dodge tools to give a three-dimensional appearance to the fur (**Fig.07** – Step 4). Finally, to give movement to the image, I added some loose fur flying in the scene (**Fig.08**).

To finish up work on the image, several textures with detailed patterns were added to the image to increase density in the painting (**Fig.09**); these textures were set to the Overlay layer blending mode. The color was then adjusted several times, and the image was finally complete (**Fig.10**).

STEP 1   STEP 2

STEP 3   STEP 4

Fig.07

CONCLUSION

It took about 100 hours in total to complete *Go forward and forward*. I've never spent that much time on any other paintings I've ever created! Even though it was difficult and time consuming, I was able to keep my initial inspiration and concept throughout the entire process. To create a good piece of work, it's not only the techniques and having a good taste in painting that are important, but also the ability to concentrate and an uncompromising stance towards your work are a necessity.

Fig.08

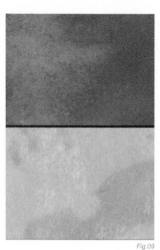
Fig.09

Fig.10

When I create new work, I usually challenge myself to learn a new technique. However, this time, I completed the image to the best of my current abilities. Instead of giving myself a challenge, I was able to stay focused single-mindedly on the painting. To challenge myself with something new is important for me in order to develop my potential, but it's also important to complete high quality work within my capabilities.

Although I only create a satisfactory image once or twice every few years, I'm very satisfied with this image and like it a lot. Fortunately, this image has also appeared on the cover of a magazine and on the cover of a CD. I'd like to use the idea of repetition and create several images as a series – my second painting of this was completed recently, but this time the subject was dogs. Hopefully, I'd like to someday have the chance to exhibit them in the near future.

ARTIST PORTFOLIO

REACHING OUT
BY SÖNKE MAETER

SOFTWARE USED: Blender and Photoshop

INTRODUCTION

This image started as an idea for an entry to the Blender World Cup challenge (bwc.blenderartists.org) for the theme, "A Moment in Time". I didn't have a concrete concept; there was just the illustration of an Asian flare provided, and a distant view in my mind ... which was probably because I'd just enjoyed playing the final part of the *Prince of Persia* trilogy. There were about two months until the challenge deadline, which gave me plenty of time to develop the image through the process of creating it. Whilst browsing through images on the internet, a reproduction of the painting of *The Tower of*

SOURCE: WIKIPEDIA

Fig.01

Babylon by Pieter Brueghel the Elder popped onto my screen, and it was clear from that moment that I wanted to create a scene with just such a grand construction (**Fig.01**).

MODELING

I started with the upper part of the tower, to get a feel for the scene and to see whether it would work to extend the likes of Breughel's Tower of Babylon to create more room for interpretation. I showed the young tower to some others, which at this stage was very reminiscent of *The Tower of Babylon*, and most of them recognized it (**Fig.02**). This made me feel sure that I was on the right track.

With a clear image of the tower in mind, I moved onto creating the city. The buildings were straightforward blocks with holes in them, so it didn't take me too long

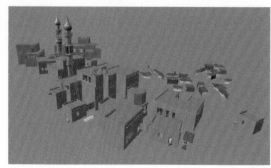

Fig.02

Fig.03

to create six unique houses and two small towers, from which I assembled the city by duplicating the different buildings several times. To make it look more appealing, I applied a different scale and rotation to them, and I used the very same method to create the foreground wall and tower from just a single stone (**Fig.03**).

Simple buildings weren't enough, however, for an interesting city, and so I had to create something for the eye to focus on as it moves over the city. This was the point at which I saw an image of the Taj Mahal; despite the fact that it's a mausoleum, I was inspired to start work building a palace to reside in the city (**Fig.04**). After some playing around with extensions to the back of the palace, I decided to stick to the initial design, simply because it suited the style of the city the best (**Fig.05 – 07**).

Fig.04

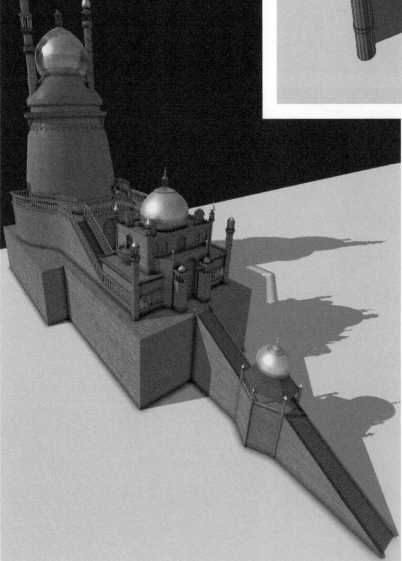

Fig.06

Fig.05

I figured that the horizon also needed something to draw attention to it, and what's more appropriate for a huge scale project having supplies delivered, such as the construction of a large tower, than a harbor (**Fig.08**)?

The only real challenge I encountered was modeling the dress of the woman, as I wasn't sure what it is that makes a dress look like a dress. But with some input from the community, and Blender's sculpting tools, I was able to create something that looked good enough (**Fig.09**).

COMPOSITION

Probably the most interesting part of this image to create and think about was the composition. After figuring out where to put the big tower and the basic foreground elements, the image looked unbalanced. There was simply too much tower on the right hand side, and there was the need for the smaller tower in the foreground. The small tower then gave me the opportunity to create a connection between the foreground and the big tower via a rope, which also has the wonderful side effect of explaining why the balloon stays put!

At this point, the only things that prevented the eye from moving in circles around the image were the triangular shapes of the wall. Figuring out the solution for this took me about five days, as I was stuck with the idea that I would have to change the triangular shapes somehow. But all of a sudden, when I was driving innocently to university, a jack-hammer started smashing something really hard, and there the idea of the iron rails linking up the stone triangles was born. It was effective, simple and more importantly: subtle (**Fig.10a – b**). Another feature that happened more by accident than thinking it through!

The image had made some progress at this stage, and I was starting to think about whether I wanted to go with cheesy romantic clouds or a sky painted by the wind (of course, I chose the latter). Whilst looking through some texture websites, I found a nice photograph of a sky on

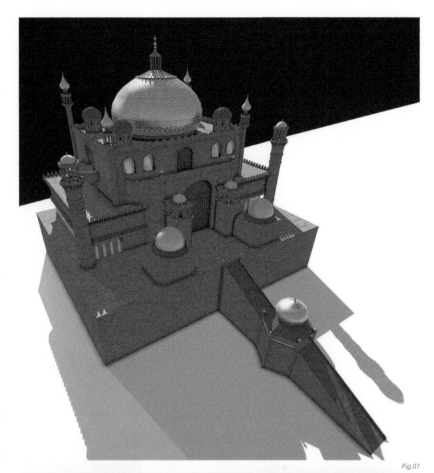

Fig.07

Fig.08

Fig.09

cgtextures.com with nice open clouds at the top, showing the blue sky – which by the way creates a great balance to the brown stone colors. So I added the picture to the render and recognized a dark spot in the clouds, shaped much like a long horizontal triangle, close to the woman's head. Editing the sky a bit created this wonderful subtle contrast between the back of her head and her face (**Fig.11**). Later on, I also recognized a stretched U-shape in the clouds; I adjusted the rotation of the big tower so that a part of the spiral staircase extended the shape (**Fig.12**).

Parts of the image were created by plain construction and following my intuition, whilst other parts simply "happened". Of course, without recognizing the different shapes and adjusting the image elements according to them, only the level of detail would've been increased. However, by creating connections through the composition of the rather unconnected elements of the image, I achieved a much more harmonious look and feel.

CONCLUSION

With my few previous pieces I lost interest throughout the process and had to be quite disciplined to finish them. In contrast, *Reaching Out* was a piece I enjoyed right from the very beginning through to the end.

Seeing how composition can affect the image quality, and how it can work for you to integrate different elements into the scene, was an enlightening experience and will also influence my future creations. I still need to work on my skills to create nice textures and lighting, and I'm also missing experience in general, but with time there will come knowledge, and I might even spend some more hours on this piece trying to improve it in the future.

Fig.10a

Fig.10b

Fig.11

Fig.12

Artist Portfolio

TRIP TO THE SOUK
BY ANDRZEJ SYKUT

SOFTWARE USED: 3d Studio Max, Wings 3D, ZBrush and Photoshop

INTRODUCTION

Trip to the Souk was, in large part, inspired by my childhood memories; I spent a few years in Tobruk, Libya, as a child and I wanted to incorporate some of those memories into an image I was creating for a contest. Why the souk theme, you ask? Well, the task was to depict human-alien relations of some kind. I

didn't really want to create a battle scene, even though it was my initial idea for the contest brief; I wanted to do something a bit different.

LAYOUT & MODELING

I'll be brief about the layout and modeling stages and focus on the post-production instead. Proper planning and pre-visualization allowed

© Andrzej Sykut

me to create the image in quite a short time. I set up
the camera and main lighting using a very simple
scene consisting of just some boxes. Since I wanted an
unusual, somewhat Escher-inspired panoramic camera

Fig.01

Fig.02

with a curved perspective, I had to do some experimenting. Angling both streets in just the right way was as important as my camera settings (V-Ray's Spherical Camera) – it's by no means a 90 degree corner (**Fig.01** – my starting point, sketch and base scene).

Models were created using Wings 3D and ZBrush, and then dropped into the basic scene with boxes; I refined it piece by piece. The scene setup was done in 3d Studio Max. The main character, the guy in the red jacket, is the same character I used in my two previous images – an explorer of some kind. I wanted to place him in the image to maintain continuity with my other works, like snapshots from his journeys around the galaxy. The other characters were quite simple models; detailed and posed in ZBrush (I wouldn't be able to do it any other way – not enough time). To render the scene, I used V-Ray (**Fig.02** – the raw render).

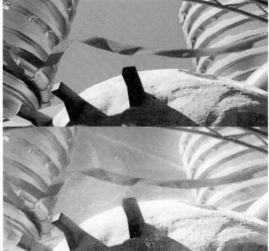

Fig.03

POST-PRODUCTION

Why is post-production crucial for an image like this? Well, let's take a look at the raw, rendered image – it's not what I wanted to achieve, or at least not yet. The colors are wrong, the exposure is not right (shadows are way too dark). There's not even a hint of atmosphere – no depth, other than what the perspective and geometry suggest. Certain objects lack detail, texture, the sky is too plain ... the list could go on and on. What's even more important is that there's no mood, no style. The viewer's eye could use some guidance around the image, too. The main characters could be more in focus; some places could be toned down a bit ... Of course, I could fix most of those issues right in the 3D software, but it would have taken much more time than I had for the contest. Doing it in Photoshop was faster and much more flexible. I did expect this, and I even planned for it, so I prepared a lot of passes: occlusions, flat color, multiple fogs, volumetrics, masks ... but since post-production is a creative process I also found that I needed additional passes that I hadn't anticipated using.

The sky started as a VRay sky. I added a subtle moon, some contrails extracted from photos, and I also added some gradient to darken the top part of the sky. Later on I made some color corrections, matching the sky with the rest of the image (**Fig.03** – the sky, before and after post-production).

I multiplied the occlusion pass over the image at a low opacity and layer-masked it so that it added detail but did not spoil anything. It's very easy to overdo this part so I had to be careful. I made the right side of the image darker, to better portray the mood I had in mind; I wanted it to look like a cold, dark, damp backstreet, in contrast with the left, sunny and hot side. Since some parts needed texture detail, I rendered additional passes

Fig.04

of textures for the offending objects; it was mostly a patterned fabric. For the curtains, I used grayscale photos of wrinkled fabric to add some more cloth-like detail (**Fig.04** – additional texture passes).

Even more detail was added with purely 2D texture overlays; some subtle dirt was applied over the whole image, as well as some more localized, specific things (mostly old, decaying walls). One of the overlay layers (a photo of an old rusted metal sheet – an old favorite of mine) produced a nice reddish cast on the cobbles, which wasn't planned but I immediately liked it (**Fig.05** – some overlay textures).

Using a raw reflection pass I added some moisture to the cobblestone street surface, which was intended from the very beginning. I then took the occlusion, normals, diffuse and fresnel passes, and used them to add selective edge/rim lights (**Fig.06a** – before, **Fig.06b** – after, and the edge light shown on its own **Fig.06c**). This is quite simple: I choose one of the channels from the normals pass, with light coming from the direction I want. Next I multiply it with the Fresnel pass so it's visible mostly on the edges. Then I multiply the occlusion over it to simulate some shadows, and multiply the whole thing with the diffuse color pass. The only things left

Fig.05

to do after are the color correction, masking of the resulting pass and then adding or screen-blending it over the image. It can work wonders to separate the planes, pop the characters out of the background, or subtly change material properties! Besides all this, I simply like subtle edge light; it can look a bit like sky reflection, or like a "peach-fuzz" layer on cloth, and it's not always practical to do in 3D. Around this time I also created a luminance mask, which I used to brighten up the shadows a touch (with a Curves adjustment layer).

The atmosphere consists of three main parts (**Fig.07** – atmospheric components, smoke, volumetrics and particles):

- **Live-action smoke** – I used filmed/photographed smoke, screen-blended over certain parts of the image
- **3D and 2D volumetrics and fogs** – which include light rays, distance fog, ground fog and 2D light rays from Trapcode Shine light effect plugin
- **3D particles** – to simulate some bigger chunks of garbage floating around in the air

Fig.06a

Fig.06b

All of the above was layer masked to appear only exactly where needed. Some of the atmospherics came in as grayscale, so they needed tinting. This is important when using screen blending mode, otherwise the image will get gray and flat very quickly. Using photographic smoke gives the image a nice, organic feel – and saves me from having to simulate it in 3D.

Next, I did some painting. I added some variation to the fruits and grain sacks, fixed some minor bugs, and added

Fig.07

Fig.06c

some highlights here and there. From then on there were mostly global look and feel edits. I added a few layers of vignettes – I kept adding them until I was happy; they nicely darkened the corners of the image. In tandem with the bright atmosphere they added a lot of depth to the scene, too. I also made the right hand part even darker and toned down the contrast. Color correction was done using adjustment layers, masked in certain areas. With all those overlays and tinted atmospherics, the corrections I needed to do were simple and quite subtle. Nice, rich colors happened somewhat by themselves, while I was working on other things.

For the final touches I painted in some glows in areas of highlights, which supplemented the smoke and dense atmosphere nicely. I added some grain, and after collapsing the layers added a tiny bit of chromatic aberration to make the edges less sharp (the trick is to rotate one of the channels by a tiny fraction, like 0.1 of a degree – just so the aberration is slightly visible in the corners of the image).

CONCLUSION

Now, let's take a look at the final image. There's nice depth, the colors are rich, and there's more focus on the characters, especially the main ones; dark corners do not drag the attention away from the central parts of the image; the atmosphere is dense, full of smoke and light – just as I imagined it to be.

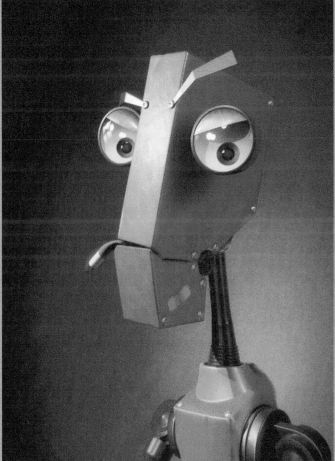

CONTAINMENT BREACH SUB-LEVEL 5

BY BRADFORD RIGNEY

SOFTWARE USED: Photoshop 7

CONCEPT

First of all, let me say how much of an honor it is to be a part of this book. I never dreamed my work would ever be included alongside such gifted artists. I guess I've always considered myself to be a fan first and an artist second, so to be sitting here writing an overview of my own work feels pretty weird. I also sincerely want to thank whoever may be reading this for taking interest in my art and for taking the time to read something that a hopeless goofball like me would set to paper (seriously, just look at my portrait).

The concept for this work was a simple one: terror. My work doesn't have any kind of deep meaning attached to it, and that's intentional; I want my concepts to be primitive, high-impact and accessible. Life, death, sexuality and fear are all themes that I'm obsessed with capturing, probably due to my exposure to Richard Corben and Frank Frazetta, who are both my larger-than-life heroes, at a very young age. What Frazetta and Corben do for me is instill a sense of cinema; a "suspension of disbelief", and a sense that what I'm seeing exists and has history. They transported me to other worlds, and I decided early on in my drawing career that I wanted my work to have that effect, too.

For this particular work, I was shooting for a tangible sense of dread, of chaos and hopelessness, of being trapped in a predator's gaze with no way of escape. I also wanted a mysterious, subterranean, sci-fi flavor to be immediate, which prompted the title. In addition to all this, I wanted to hint at the theme of mankind tampering with things he shouldn't, which is why I put what could be interpreted as a "contained" specimen of the monster in a sort of cryo-embryo-tank over there on the right hand side of the composition. The idea of mankind paying horrifically for his scientific ambitions was always a cool cliché in sci-fi, I thought, and incorporating that idea here was definitely a goal. I also can't stress enough that, as a child of the 80s, I've survived on a steady diet of horror movies, *Creepy* magazine, D&D and death metal. Inevitably all of that thick, yummy goodness gets distilled into my ideas and this one isn't any different.

THE MAKING OF CONTAINMENT BREACH SUB-LEVEL 5

I'm a failed 3D modeler, crappy oil painter and self-taught illustrator, so hopefully what I have to offer will be useful to those of you who are trained, and won't be too far off-course for those of you who aren't. Much of what I do is intuition-based, while capitalizing on any happy mistakes.

I don't ever use reference material, but I will look at a few photos to make sure the hand-drawn result is accurate. Everything is done from start to finish in Photoshop 7, using a Wacom tablet. Basically, I start off with a warm or cool base and lay down big blobs of dark value with a huge brush set at around 40% opacity. I then apply a radial blur or motion blur – sometimes both – and work the movement until I have something that "feels good". After I have a "stage" set on the canvas, I lay down figures in the general poses that "feel right", with a smaller brush (of the same opacity). Once the figures are arranged, I make a duplicate layer and save it, so I can work on the duplicate without losing what I have. With the basics down, I begin to add more value with the same brush, using the history brush to shape the figures and scenery until the idea becomes less nebulous. The end result (**Fig.01**) is a skeleton for the next "phase", which is the lighting.

The next phase (**Fig.02**) is all about laying in both color and light, usually with a smaller brush (set at the same

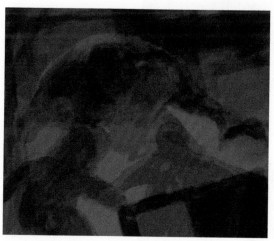

Fig.01

40% opacity) and a large dodge tool set at around 16% for highlights, emphasizing the light source while using the history brush to control where it falls. For this work I knew I wanted soft backlighting, strong under-lighting and harsh rim-lights, a classic horror movie scheme.

At this point (**Fig.03**) I've made strong thematic changes. Initially, I wanted the foreground figures to be lab-coat scientists. But once the work started to evolve, it seemed right to put them in hazmat suits which I felt made them more fragile. This was also to imply that the viewer is a part of this containment team, with the first-person view taken into consideration while one of the victims engages the viewer. At this point, I hunt for photographs

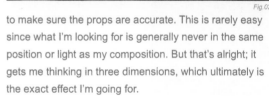

Fig.02

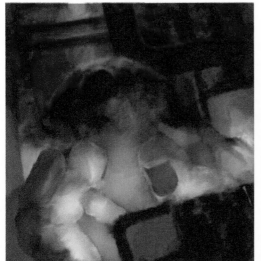

Fig.03

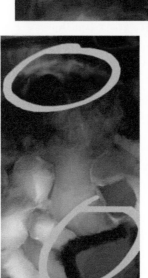

Fig.04

to make sure the props are accurate. This is rarely easy since what I'm looking for is generally never in the same position or light as my composition. But that's alright; it gets me thinking in three dimensions, which ultimately is the exact effect I'm going for.

The next step is the meat and potatoes. Probably the most important tool I use is the smudge tool, which I keep set to around 40%. If you take a close look (**Fig.04**) you can see where I basically use the smudge tool to "sculpt" the pixels into place. From here until the finish, I'll be using that very smudge tool technique in addition to the dodge, lasso and history brushes, with regular paintbrushes to refine the work.

Now comes the critical phase (**Fig.05**): finalizing body language, expressions, anatomy, evolving the foci and detailing. This is the most time consuming and rewarding aspect of the process. Comparing this phase (**Fig.05**) with the end result, you can see where many structural changes took place, particularly to scale, expressions and attitude. These changes are of critical importance to my goal of eliciting sympathy for the victims and fear of the monster.

The camcorder screen (**Fig.06**) was created by selecting an area of the creature and running it through a channel mixer to get a "video" look. Then I selected bands of the

Fig.05

screen and ran them through various filters (motion blur, shear and mezzotint) to ideally achieve an interrupted signal effect. The symbols are hand-drawn while the lettering is done with the text tool. Finally, a film grain is added.

Once everything feels finished, I merge all layers, then jack up the saturation and contrast before finally applying an unsharp-mask filter to make it all "pop".

CONCLUSION

So did I succeed in creating a creepy, high-impact horror piece?

That's something I'd like to leave up to you to decide.

Fig.06

ARTIST PORTFOLIO

DETECTIVE'S OFFICE
BY CRAIG SELLARS

SOFTWARE USED: Photoshop CS2

INTRODUCTION

The principal inspiration for this image was derived from the subject matter and moody compositions of film noir and the period settings of the paintings of Edward Hopper. With these influences in mind, I set out to create an image which would also contain a juxtaposition of some sort that would provide an interesting twist and imply all sorts of story to the finished image.

I had the idea to create a scene depicting a staple of the film noir genre, the detective's office. I figured there were a lot of rich cues from this type of location I could use, such as the warm hues and period items like telephones and horizontal window blinds. Now, because I wanted to

blend imagery to make this scene seem a little more fantastic, I started to think about what else I could place in this scene. I began bouncing around the idea of a 40s pulp style robot, perhaps standing by the window with light streaming through the blinds casting lines of shadow across his body. This would be a very heavy handed mixing of visual cues and I began to think about what, or whom, else I could incorporate into this scene.

I decided I wanted to have a group of figures interacting in this environment and use their staging to help tell the story. Thinking back to a lot of pulp illustrations, there was often a detective and the woman he was working for portrayed in precarious situations. I decided this was the

to create dramatic lighting, I started in grayscale. This method is beneficial when you really want to have strong lighting and composition because you can focus on the graphic shapes and the values without being concerned with hue and texture yet. I started by filling the canvas with a mid-tone gray to use as my ground to paint into. Using the Airbrush hard round brush (from the default Photoshop brush set), I began sketching out the staging of the man, woman and the robot (**Fig.01**).

Fig.01

route to follow: focus on the man and woman and let the robot fall into the background and be "discovered" by the viewer.

PROCESS

With my core idea of the illustration figured out I began to sketch. I was going for a cinematic feel so I used a canvas with a screen proportion. Because I wanted

Fig.02

Fig.03

I liked the idea of a bit of an upshot. (Old films often used what were, at the time, unorthodox camera angles such as a tilt or an upshot showing the ceiling. These angles would put what were ordinary situations, such as two characters talking, into a new context for the viewer.)

As I blocked in the characters I very quickly started to imply the lighting for the scene (**Fig.02**). In the spirit of film noir, I really wanted to let things fall into shadow, so I started to establish a single light source

above the characters, yet slightly behind them so they catch a nice rim light. As a result, the foreground figures are dimly lit only by reflected light from the rest of the room.

Next, I turned my attention to the poor neglected robot in the back of the room. I begin refining his shape and defining the window casing behind him, which I used as a compositional framing element (**Fig.03**). I implied the horizontal blinds, though I decided against having light stream

Fig.04

through them as I wanted to rely only on the single modest light to illuminate my scene.

Working around the image as a whole, I started to rough in other elements, such as the desk, and loosely imply period architectural elements on the left, behind the characters. At this point I knew that this illustration was about the interaction of the characters, therefore most of the background was only loosely implied. I also moved back to the robot to make him a little more imposing, in both scale and design (**Fig.04**).

Next I started to add color. This was done quickly by creating an Overlay layer and painting in a warm overall hue, sort of keying the painting to a particular color. I knew that I wanted to keep the color range pretty narrow, so at this point I added most of the local color, which was the man's suit and the woman's dress (**Fig.05a**).

Fig.05a

Also at this stage, I knocked the upper part of the robot into shadow. This tends to make the robot feel backed up against the wall and as if he is hiding in the shadows (**Fig.05b**). Lighting compositions like this were used widely in film noir and add a lot of subtle narrative to an image.

Once the color was in place I quickly went in to better define all the characters. I then used a couple of custom brushes to add texture and a little more interest to the scene (**Fig.06**). At this point I made sure that the values were working well, paying particular attention to the primary focus of the scene – the sitting woman. In addition to tweaking the drawing and cleaning up her silhouette, I made sure the highlights were falling in a realistic way and the play of light was interesting and convincing. The robot was pretty lonely back there, so I added a vague figure next to him. What is he doing there? Well, that is up to the viewer to decide.

Next, I worked the finishing touches. I added some highlights here and there (**Fig.07a – c**), and then painted on an Overlay layer a golden hue to warm the image up, particularly in the areas of light. Finally, using the Levels editor in Photoshop to adjust the overall values of the

Fig.05b

Fig.06

image, I made the light areas a bit brighter and darkened the mid tones. This created more overall contrast. And with these final touches, the image was finished.

CONCLUSION

I felt that, based on my original inspiration and goals, this was a pretty successful image. There could have been a few more secondary points of interest that were described with more detail … Perhaps I could have been a bit heavier handed with the light streaming through those blinds, or implied more of a stark environment as Hopper did in his work? I was pleased with the lighting,

Fig.07a

Fig.07b

Fig.07c

particularly the backlight and rim lighting of the woman and the story/drama that it implies. Like the woman, the lighting on the robot was also successful. Dropping him halfway into the shadows implied he was intimidated, which was in contrast to his imposing appearance and allowed the viewer to discover the odd participant in this scene.

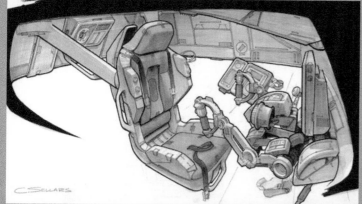

Saving the Alien Girl
By Daniel Lieske

SOFTWARE USED: ZBrush and Photoshop

INTRODUCTION

Online art contests frequently motivate me to put a huge amount of effort into a single artwork. This very thing happened with *Saving the Alien Girl*, which was created for the "Uplift Universe CGChallenge" on CGTalk. I also had another strong motivation for this project, however; after having played around with ZBrush for several months and only having produced experimental images during this time, I finally wanted to find out if I could produce a full scale artwork using only ZBrush and Photoshop. I'm not a 3D artist so to speak, and I think I also wanted to find out how "3D" you can get without actually starting with a classic 3D software package. You're looking at the outcome of this experiment, which took me nearly eight weeks' worth of long evenings and busy weekends.

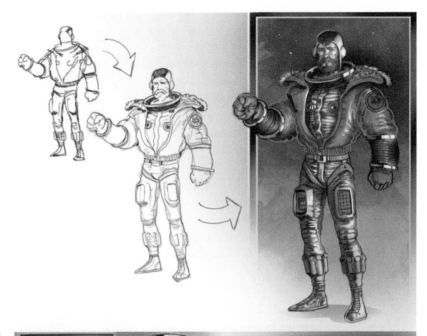

Fig.02

Fig.03

Fig.01

SKETCHES

I work in 2D most of the time, and so my natural way to work is to sketch things out before I spend a lot of time on the details. **Fig.01** shows some sketches of the hero character done in Photoshop. I also like to do quick color sketches like the ones you can see in **Fig.02**. I normally use these to work out compositions or, like in the case of the alien girl, for concept art, if color is an important aspect of the design.

Since I worked mainly in ZBrush I also experimented with the possibilities of sketching in 3D. **Fig.03** shows an early scene layout for which I roughly modified a human base mesh into the right proportions for the different characters. This gave me the interesting opportunity to experiment with the scene from different viewing angles.

SCULPTING

I began sculpting with the monster (**Fig.04**). I jumped right into its design from the roughly modeled human base mesh. ZBrush is great at blocking in form and so I did not create any sketches of the monster's appearance – just went on with my inspiration. I sculpted the monster directly in his pose, which caused a lot of work because I wasn't able to use the symmetry functions this way. After the form of the monster detached more and more from human proportions, I realized that the original base mesh did not hold the details of the beast anymore. So I had to retopologize it – also without symmetry – which took over 15 hours. The final model of the monster had over 6 million polygons.

I sculpted the girl in a T-pose, which made it a lot quicker and easier for me (**Fig.05**). The cloth geometry was extracted from the girl's surface after she was transposed into her final pose, and was then sculpted in pose. The hero character was also sculpted in a T-pose (**Fig.06**). He was composed of several SubTools which made the posing a bit complicated. Fortunately, I did not have to retopologize him as well.

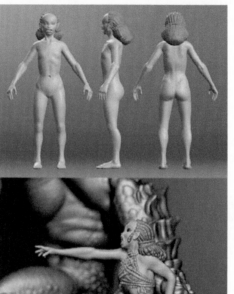
Fig.04

Fig.05   *Fig.06*

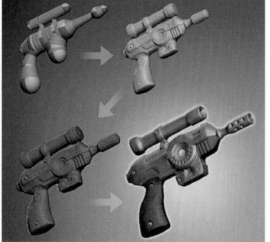
Fig.07

Fig.08

After the characters I detailed the tree trunk and modeled the hero's blaster pistol. Both were initially created with ZSpheres and for the tree trunk the automatic adaptive skin worked perfectly and I could sculpt the details right away (**Fig.07**). For the blaster I had to create a new topology over the rough blocked-in sculpting to straighten out the edges (**Fig.08**).

All the different objects of the foreground scene were organized as SubTools inside ZBrush and brought my humble PC to its limits. All SubTools together had over 13 million polygons and I was glad when all the sculpting was done and I was able to drop everything to the 2.5D canvas (but before that comes the painting).

PAINTING

I painted all objects using ZBrush's poly painting function (**Fig.09**). Here, again, ZBrush is absolutely straightforward as there is no need to create any UV coordinates. You just paint on the model and you're done. Painting the models was quite quick and fun, and I made plenty of use of the cavity masking feature which allows you to paint only the peaks of the geometry on the one hand (much like dry brushing in traditional model painting), or lets the paint sink into the creases on the other.

BUILDING THE SCENE

Once all the foreground objects were sculpted and painted, I arranged them on ZBrush's 2.5D canvas. This meant that the angles of the objects could not be altered anymore but it gave me the possibility to add a lot more detail to the scene. All the moss, little plants and branches on the tree trunk were added to the scene on the 2.5D canvas. For the background I created separate documents in which I arranged the hills, the planets (**Fig.10**) and the mid-ground trees (**Fig.11**). For these trees I used the Deco Brush in ZBrush which allows you to paint with a texture which is dynamically transformed along the stroke path. Using this technique it is possible to create complex floral designs in mere minutes.

COMPOSITING

ZBrush's 2.5D canvas is essentially a 2D canvas with added depth information. Once an object is dropped onto the 2.5D canvas, it is translated into pixel information. Every pixel still knows his position in the image depth and so it's possible to relight the whole image, although it's not a 3D scene. However, just like a 3D artist, I created different light passes from the image and composed them in Photoshop. **Fig.12** shows some of the passes that were created from the ZBrush document, including several light passes, a diffuse color pass and an ambient occlusion shadow pass (**A** – Final Composite, **B** – Rim Light, **C** – Special Material, **D** – Specular, **E** – Special Material, **F** – GI Shadows, **G** – Color, **H** – Combined Lights). All these passes were then combined and tweaked

Fig.09

in Photoshop. After adding the clouds and using Richard Rosenman's Depth of Field Pro plugin for some defocus in the foreground and background, the artwork was finally done.

CONCLUSION

I'm quite happy with the result of my experiment. For me it's a very unconventional artwork considering my portfolio. The 3D sculpting allowed for a huge level of detail here and there, maybe even a bit too much? However, the main point for me is that I had all the cool stuff which comes with 3D, like different light passes and the perfect rendering of form, but did not have to worry at all about polygon modeling tools, material editors, shader trees or rendering options. ZBrush is quite straightforward in all these fields and feels more like enhanced painting, and not so much like 3D rendering. This is definitely a workflow I will use in the future and which I can recommend to anyone who wants to experiment with 3D, but hesitates to touch one of the big 3D software packages.

Fig.10

Fig.11

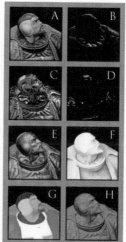

Fig.12

ARTIST PORTFOLIO

All Images © Daniel Lieske

CAPSULA
BY EDUARDO PEÑA

SOFTWARE USED: Photoshop CS3

INTRODUCTION

To share the creation process of this dream-like world with you, I would first of all like to point out the factors that made it possible for me to enjoy it. I find it important as an artist to understand and to continue exploring the visual language that I encounter on a daily basis; enriching and building it up in order to better understand my needs as an artist. It's also important to be able to understand your personal inclinations in order to depict your aesthetic criteria in this marvelous art and design discipline. In the case of my work, it is the subject of science-fiction that I lean towards.

For me, it's essential to understand what it is that one desires to experience. An image is capable of expressing emotion; it can intervene with the senses to create an atmosphere that can trap and expose a rich narrative which communicates with us, affecting our feelings and perceptions towards a visual piece.

Before entering technically into the creation of a new image, I always imagine that I am the protagonist of a situation in a distant and curious context; I try to think, and even live, a hundred percent in that space – I breathe the air, I feel the climate, I abandon my senses and explore what surrounds me. I also love to play music in this kind of situation. Music is such an important element that articulates and invigorates my experiences.

CONCEPT

For *Capsula*, I decided to create a crossing in a distant future, far away from prejudice but full of benevolent mysteries. I am a pilot, an explorer; I'm walking towards a strange vehicle. I'm walking calmly, as if the motion is part of my everyday life, something that I always do with great pleasure. There's a lot of metal surrounding me; it's a strange climate, the light is very intense, the air is very dense, but there is coolness in the environment … Thinking in this manner, I was already beginning to define what my chromatic palette could be, and the types of line that I would use to build up the fictitious world – which is in fact simply a translation made from my experience with the formal world which I actually inhabit.

WORKFLOW

For most images I don't tend to use a defined formula; I'm constantly exposed to a good dose of experimentation in my work, since the virtual medium allows me to take

Fig.01

advantage of this perfectly. There are times that I begin with "accidents", other times by using some classic rules of composition. In this case I decided to start with a common tool: some perspective lines that would help me to work out the composition I wanted to elaborate upon. What perspective does is to help me organize the objects in a three-dimensional environment. Once these parameters were established, I started work.

I started with some forms and indefinite spots, playing with accidents to see what could happen (**Fig.01**). The process was very enjoyable; I was literally playing, and that's where the process is so important: it's where you decide your strokes, spots and lines, trying to organize them – not to limit their expressive powers, but to visually nourish a great idea! Strokes and textures are versatile; they allowed me to play and permitted me to think about what I really had in mind, carving it little by little until my head told my hand, "Good, that should be the way to do

Fig.02

Fig.03

Fig.04a

Fig.04b

it!" I continued the translation process, generally trying to maintain total equilibrium in the work.

Most of the time I work in black and white, for both comfort as well as to be able to establish contrast and value before the color maelstrom (however, this is all very relative according to the needs of the moment). So, continuing with the accidental and structured construction of the piece, I carried on consolidating the form and the visual force that was going to project the image (**Fig.02**). I tried to leave references aside as much as possible and relied upon my own natural software, my head, to make the process more interesting. I believe that to think and to imagine is more enriching, helping you to leave aside prejudice and really enjoy what you're doing.

Little by little I defined the space, implying objects and structures in different areas of the composition in order to better describe something of the context where everything was happening. I also started building the central part up, with the initial form of the transport having been conceived (**Fig.03**), which could be something mechanical, robotic.

In this phase of the image creation my head started calling for color, it was almost like a biological need: I want to see color. I applied a layer of color, using the Colorize option, introducing a layer of texture as an experiment. Through this, I acquired some textures and interesting forms that helped the visual richness of the

Fig.05

image (**Fig.04a – b**). This method is also a good way of helping to build new proposals that, at the time, we may not have thought of previously. It's always necessary to experience many different forms, to constantly create new methods of construction.

There's obviously nothing new in the way I am presenting this work to you, but the way in which you use and take advantage of this information for something more personal is down to you; only you will know what you can take from this visual language. I'll continue creating work with a certain approach until the time I say, "Hey, that's enough!" There is always a limit. How do we know when to stop…? Well, as I've mentioned before, our natural compositions mean that we will always be our own eyes; we are the only ones that know when to stop, or when to continue (**Fig.05**).

Fig.06a

Fig.06b

Fig.07

In the majority of my works, including this one, I like
to work with the least quantity of layers possible – a
maximum of three layers. This allows me to leave
aside my insecurities and gives me the courage to take
responsibility for my errors. I continued working my
chromatic palette, with cold colors, and at the same
time carried on building all kinds of elements that surround the
image, including the ones that began in the composition
and my odd machine.

At this stage, the machine had already been defined
as a quadruped robot, but little by little I tried to give it
a more particular form, trying to make it bigger, more
impressive, but at the same time kind and harmonious.
This was a pleasing contrast, since I didn't want to show
anything of aggression in the environment (**Fig.06a – b**);
I find that the circular form gives it a more organic touch,
and for this I got inspiration from the scientific expedition
submarines (**Fig.07**). The machine, as well as a means
of transportation, is an exploration vehicle. It is large

Fig.08

because, on the trip I'm planning to take, I want to go somewhere far away from technology. Perhaps it might need some kind of extra help to get me there? … We'll see.

As a final touch, I added some finishing details and felt happy calling the piece complete (**Fig.08 – 09**).

CONCLUSION

I very much enjoy visualizing stories, bringing them to life on my canvas and creating a history of work that I can obviously continue into the future. Finally, I hope this has been pleasing for you to read; I'm thankful for your attention.

Fig.09

ARTIST PORTFOLIO

STATION C43
By James Paick

SOFTWARE USED: Photoshop CS2

INTRODUCTION

With the rush of day to day work, I try to find different outlets that allow me to create new personal work. Not long ago, an opportunity presented itself when Kevin Chen, a fellow concept artist, approached me with an opportunity to teach an environment design class. This piece was created as an in-class demonstration at the Concept Design Academy in Pasadena, California. My class focused on quick ideation with speed painting and exploration to create unique worlds for video game and film industries. The main purpose for this demo was to create a "blue sky" concept painting to help establish a look and feel of a game or film. The genre was to be very industrial and in the realm of post apocalyptic. *Station C43* was created to showcase a quick and easy way to portray a convincing concept, story and mood.

WORKFLOW

The initial steps are very important when starting a painting. I do not draw the first thing that comes to mind; however, I do know what genre, story and mood I want to portray. I personally like to start off by putting down large brushstrokes to tone the canvas and establish a basic composition. I like to use some custom brushes with

Fig.01a   Fig.01b

texture to start off the painting. Many people like to work in a grayscale; however, I like to work in color to set up a tone from the beginning. Using the lasso tool is a great way to create shapes (hotkey L). After a short while, I begin to see an interesting shape that I can start building from (**Fig.01a – b**).

With a solid starting point, I begin to plug in elements to establish a foreground, middle and background (**Fig.02**). These elements are important when dealing with a large scale environment and are important to address in an early stage. One way I address the scale issue is by allowing my major shape to be a strong, readable and distinct silhouette. I surround the major shape with many supporting elements, smaller buildings, towers, bridges and so on to help push the size and scale comparison. Allowing the viewer to identify a scale figure, a person, car or trees is great to use to establish an immediate scale reference.

Fig.02

Fig.03

With the cool tones set by my initial lay-in, my next step is to establish a warm/cool relationship in light and shadow temperature (**Fig.03**). I start off by using the lasso tool to create shapes that represent the ground and side planes of the floor, building and other surrounding elements. With the selection made, I paint in a warmer and lighter tone to represent direct light. The lighting creates a focal point with the positioning of contrasting values and color. The ideal placement for a focal area is to be pushed off-center. To make sense of the warm light filtering into the environment, I start to paint in sky elements with a dark, overcast sky on the right with a break in the clouds on the left to make sense of the lighting scheme.

Now I want to start bringing this piece to life. I want to portray this area to be an industrial factory area, so the shape language should be appropriate to the concept. I go out to local refineries, power plants and industrial strips to take photographs and gather references. The references I gather can help me build a very convincing and realistic environment by using photographic overlays as a basis to paint on top of. My logic is to have the greatest amount of detail in and around the focal area.

Fig.04

This allows the piece to have very tight and resolved areas with other loosely painted elements together. At the base of the structure, I overlay photographic texture to help describe the facades and mass of the building. This helps me to immediately establish the amount of detail the rest of the piece needs. I also start to define the rest of the silhouette shapes of the main structure and repeat the same process that was used at the base of the building (**Fig.04**).

Many people ask me how I create such large and epic environments. The trick is in how your represent scale. It helps to establish the scope and the viewer can really get a sense of the massive world you create! Something I do to show scale is to repeat shapes throughout the environment – it's the same thought process as telephone poles down a street. I establish a shape language, texture and proportions of the main structure and want to repeat the shapes in other places in the background. I also keep in mind to resolve the ground plane; tighten up the major perspective lines and sky. I

Fig.05

don't want to pay equal attention to all details throughout the piece; I reserve the tight detailed areas for the focal point (**Fig.05**).

I am happy with the lighting, color and composition. When these factors are working well together, I move my attention to the smaller details and resolve the piece. The attention to detail is to make sure my forms are reading correctly and resolve the color and lighting. I like to push the warm tones where the light and shadow meet together as well as portions of the sky (**Fig.06a – b**). At this point, all my buildings in the mid- and background have proper form description, lighting and color.

Depicting a story is an important part of a concept. To show my story, I introduced some characters. These military soldiers on patrol show a storyline that immediately sets the tone for the piece. This also helps the eye to travel around the composition. With the

Fig.06a

Fig.06b

addition of other elements, such as flying ships, smoke and windows, the piece starts to pull together nicely (**Fig.06c**).

The finishing touches can be made now. Much of the architecture needs to be revisited and touched up. There are also small perspective issues that need to be resolved, as well as making any adjustments to values and colors. I have to remember that I reserve my darker values for the foreground and let the values lighten further back in space (**Fig.07**).

Fig.06c

CONCLUSION

Overall, I am happy with this piece. The steps that were taken to produce this image were simple and effective. It met all my goals that I set out for it. I wanted to create an environment that was concept driven and convincingly portrayed with solid fundamental art application. These are the steps I take with a majority of my work. There are no simple tricks, just hard work and practice. Now go and paint!

Fig.07

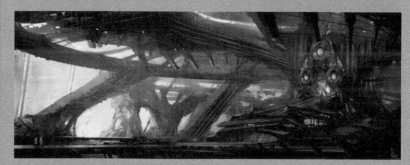

Beach Mecha
By Leonid Kozienko

SOFTWARE USED: Photoshop and Painter

Introduction

I created *Beach Mecha* in 2006. If you're unfamiliar with the term "mecha", in Japanese the word encompasses all mechanical objects. It's often used to refer to walking vehicles or humanoid robots controlled by a pilot.

For me, the creative process varies from image to image, but there are generally two ways to create an image. The first method sees you knowing exactly what you want to create – you just "see" the image in your mind. In this case the process is pretty straightforward. The second approach is more complicated: you have a feeling, rather than a complete picture in your mind; you don't know how much time you'll spend researching and producing sketches until you get the right look and feel.

Workflow

For this particular image I had no idea how it would turn out in the end. At the beginning all I had was a blank white digital canvas created in Photoshop. There are many ways that you can start a painting, but in general you'll start from a black and white sketch or go straight into a color drawing. For the digital painting I prefer to work from color and get rid of the white as soon as possible. I used the gradient tool and large textured brushes to cover the canvas with basic colors; these colors helped to establish a specific mood (a good painting always expresses some kind of mood). The textured brushes were also helpful since they could produce unexpected, interesting shapes and patterns. By looking at those random blobs my brain started to imagine things (it's really important for an artist to have a strong imagination!).

As you can see from **Fig.01** the patterns were pretty aligned and repetitive, since there was no jitter function which randomly rotated and resized the brush tip in Photoshop 6.0. But that's OK – as a digital artist you should be able to draw with anything, and thus the software shouldn't dictate how you draw. In this simple sketch I saw some sort of sunset scene, so the next step was to create a story. This was a really interesting moment since landscapes (even in such a crude form) are

Fig.01

Fig.02

just landscapes; they can convey a mood and put you into a mental state, but they unfortunately do have limited abilities in terms of telling exciting stories.

I started to block out some mechanical shapes on a new layer using a hard edge brush and simple colors that fit with the background (**Fig.02**), which is important if you want to achieve color harmony and realism in your work – in reality the environment affects everything! It's also handy to keep things in layers: by painting in layers you can easily add and subtract shapes without disturbing the background. You can also move and transform your shapes while balancing your composition.

I flipped the canvas, moved mecha to the right and added a character to the composition (**Fig.03**). I also defined the horizon line, sky and ground. You can see at this point the image was starting to tell a story, which could be something as simple as a pilot and his vehicle – or more ambitious and dramatic depending on the imagination.

I like to keep my preliminary sketches fairly small (around 1000-1200 pixels wide) to avoid unnecessary details

Fig.03

and to help speed up the process. There is always a temptation to dive into tiny details and refinement before you've established solid composition, lighting and color, but with a relatively low resolution you're forced to think in big shapes, and to concentrate on the composition and lighting first and foremost.

A good way to spark your imagination is to slap a photograph (or a few photographs) over your drawing. It could be anything from macro photography to random textures or patterns. Play with layer modes until you see something interesting. Comparing this technique to matte paintings or photo collages, these photos work as a trigger for your imagination. I used some clipart photography (I believe it was a girl laying down on a beach), set it to the Lighten layer blending mode and erased a lot of it until I found some interesting shapes (**Fig.04**).

Fig.04

At this point I came up with a story for the image. I was imagining a sunny beach with a girl enjoying the breeze and the sun. Long ago, it was a battlefield, but all that remains now is that old rusted battle mech, like an echo from the past (**Fig.05**). I thought it wouldn't be very interesting if I just painted a lady enjoying sunbathing, or a battlefield with explosions and armies of robots. It was also important to put myself into the scene: to see it, feel it – even smell it in my mind. It's very hard to create an attractive artwork if you don't have any emotional connection with it. In my personal experience I've visited places with wrecked and old ships, so I knew both how it felt and looked.

My mecha shape was already established at this stage so I started to refine its body and legs, adding bullet holes, armor panels and all that tech stuff. I added some yachts on new layers and refined the blurry horizon line into a distant city (**Fig.06**). The girl's legs and pose weren't looking too good here, so I erased some of her shape (always keep things in layers!). The girl was actually the hardest part. Understanding human form is essential and it comes with practice, so draw as much as possible!

Fig.05

Fig.06

Fig.07

Fig.07 illustrates the mask approach I used to isolate some areas in the background layer. Sometimes you can't keep everything separated out into layers but, for example, you may need to apply a filter to certain objects without affecting others. In this case you can make a selection, or paint a mask (which is actually the same thing).

I continued playing with elements in **Fig.08**, but these changes were minor. The composition was set, as well as the lighting, mood and color. However, these minor corrections required a lot of time – you get used to your images over time and eventually become tired of them. Sometimes it's useful to put your painting aside and start another one, or go out and hang out with some friends – forget about your painting for a day or two. This break will refresh you so that you can spot certain errors or

Fig.08

SCI-FI

come up with new ideas and solutions when you get back to your work. Don't force yourself too much – it's really important that you enjoy the process!

In the final stage I cleaned up areas, refined the foreground and fixed the girl's pose. I also adjusted the color levels to make the whole image brighter (**Fig.09**). The final touch-ups were then done in Painter 6.0, due to its brushes and blenders, and the image was completed there.

CONCLUSION

Looking back I can see now how I could have done it much better, technically, but the emotional response from the artwork is still satisfying. By looking at people's reactions to this image I started to realize that a good or interesting story surpasses technical flaws or issues. As an artist you can't stop progressing whilst keeping your brushes busy, so each next piece will be better than your previous one. This process is infinite. The good stories that you put into your images are timeless, so your audience will be able to experience and enjoy them year after year.

Fig.09

ARTIST PORTFOLIO

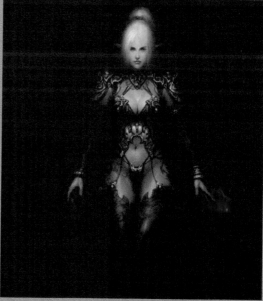

FLUID X
BY RUDOLF HERCZOG

SOFTWARE USED: Cinema 4D R10.5, Maxwell Render, Bryce 5.5 and Photoshop

INTRODUCTION

The idea for this scene came from a very rough concept based on hanging fuel pumps. I have a passion for scenes that take place in a decayed future, and with this one I wanted to create a futuristic gas station – long abandoned. Normally I have a pretty good idea of what I want to create before starting with any modeling work, but in this case I pretty much came up with the scene whilst building it. I already had the idea for the pumps so I basically built the rest around that. Often a key model can be good enough to give you enough ideas for an entire scene.

MODELING

I started out with the fuel pumps. Most of my models usually start out as basic primitives, which I then add more detail to as I go. Rather than using lots of UV maps, I prefer to model as much detail as I can and then build everything from several parts, as they would have been done in real life. It may seem somewhat tedious, but the advantage is that it makes texturing that much easier.

Once I was satisfied with the design of the pump (**Fig.01**), I started working on the main structure. Since I was thinking of incorporating some flying cars into the scene, I wanted a platform located high up in the air as part of a tower or skyscraper. I used a simple tube object for the center and started filling up the scene by building

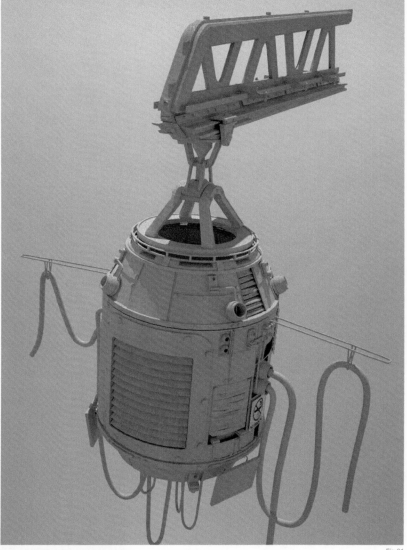

Fig.01

platforms, support beams, and fuel containers (etc.) around it; I then connected most of the objects with thick wires, pipes and bolts.

As much as I love detail work, I also like the details to have some purpose – retractable pumps, attached cables, gaps in the walkways where you park the "car" and so on (**Fig.02 – 03**). With the main structure done, I also modeled some props which I spread out on the walkways – not only to fill up the space but also to give the scene a messy look (**Fig.04 – 05**).

My initial idea was to place the scene in the center of a city surrounded by buildings and streets, but the tests I made resulted in a way too cramped scene for my tastes,

Fig.02

so I decided to add a large cityscape in the background instead. For this purpose, I went back to my old software Bryce 5.5. This program is capable of handling massive poly counts with ease, plus it would give me the distance haze needed, so I built up the entire background there using both Bryce and Cinema 4D-made models (**Fig.06**).

TEXTURING

The texturing was a fairly simple procedure. As previously mentioned, I normally model all the detail in my scenes so I didn't need to worry about creating complex maps. I could instead use tiled textures and still receive plenty of variation in the texturing if I wanted to do it that way.

I use a lot of image based materials for my scenes, and for this one I chose several metal and concrete textures from 3DTotal's Total Texture DVDs, as well as making use of a few materials specific for the Maxwell renderer. For most of the metal parts I used a galvanized material and applied some extra dirt to it using black and white dirt maps. As I wanted the construction to look really aged and weathered, I used some fairly similar materials for most of the parts (**Fig.07**).

POST-PRODUCTION

I used Maxwell to render out the Cinema 4D scene using the sun as the only light source, set at late afternoon, and rendered out an alpha mask at the same time to use

Fig.03

Fig.04

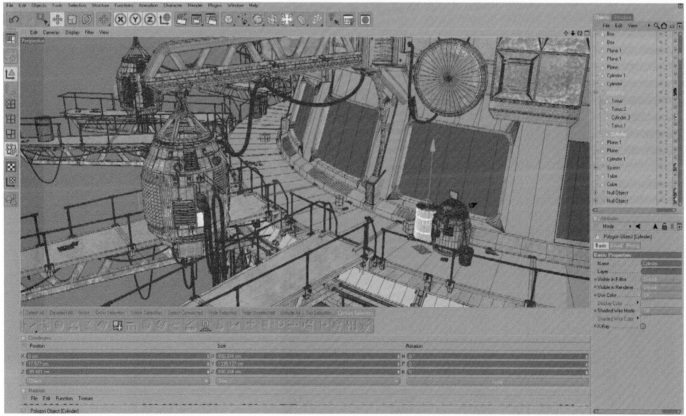

Fig.05

for the final stages. I also made a Bryce render of the city and matched the light source and camera as well as I could with the Cinema 4D scene. Once that was done I opened up both the Cinema 4D render and the background city in Photoshop, and used the alpha to erase the empty background of the station.

Two of the things I always like to pay extra attention to when it comes to post work on an image are dirt, and giving the scene a proper atmosphere. So first and foremost I matched up the two scenes properly and made a few billboard signs, as well as adding window reflections using parts of the cityscape. The next step was to take care of the colors and atmosphere.

I started out using some gamma correction to increase the contrast and enhance some of the shadows. I then made a few copies of each part and used the layer blending mode and opacity settings along with the Color Balance and Hue/Saturation adjustment tools to tweak the colors further. I used fewer colors on the background to keep the focus on the station, and added a slight Gaussian blur to the city, giving it the appearance of being far below the rest of the construction (**Fig.08**).

It was then time to dirty up the scene! For scenes like these, I try to avoid using perfectly clean materials in order to get a base to work with. A little dirt and imperfection is good, but I wanted to keep this at a low level as I have more control in applying it with post work. I used parts of several dirt maps in different blend and opacity modes and applied them to cracks, corners and smaller details, as well as larger clean surfaces. To finish

Fig.06

Fig.07

Fig.08

up the post-production, I baked all layers and added a little more gamma and color correction to complete the image (**Fig.09**).

CONCLUSION

In retrospect, there are always things you'd like to change in an image. I guess I could've spent a little more time working on the details and the coloring of the background, but still, it ended up looking way better than the initial tests and I'm quite pleased with the end result.

Fig.09

THE GOLD LIGHT OF MORNING
BY STEFAN MORRELL

SOFTWARE USED: 3d Studio Max, finalRender and Photoshop CS4

INTRODUCTION

I've always had a thing for vast sci-fi cityscapes and futuristic craft flying across imagined vistas, which I imagine comes from the great matte paintings I've seen in various films through the years. The recent matte paintings from the *Star Wars* films – Episodes 1-3 – are endlessly inspiring to me. Yusei Uesugi, Chris Stoski, Yanick Dusseault and all the great artists that worked on those shots are a huge inspiration, and I'd say a lot of what I've seen from their work has played a great influence in this piece in particular.

COMPOSITION

The initial concept for this was that of a vast cityscape being blasted by a strong golden sunrise, so I had a pretty good idea from the outset what

the final image would look like. I was going for that cool backlit effect that buildings have, where the light seems to creep around the edges of objects. I know it's all very clichéd and somewhat tacky, but I had a lot of fun making it. I also wanted strong shapes in this image and to keep the composition relatively simple to read.

MODELING

When modeling the scene I used traditional poly modeling techniques; I used 3d Studio Max, which has a great toolset available. To get this image up and running I created a basic greebled plane and instanced it several times – it's about a mile in length and was then rotated, scaled and some faces were deleted, all in an effort to tile it across the scene and keep it from looking repetitious. The Greeble plugin is available

for free, so most people are familiar with it. One major drawback in using this plugin, however, is that it looks very obvious: one can very easily tell if something's been greebled because of the generic shapes it creates.

To augment the greebled sheets I also modeled some low-res "city blocks" (**Fig.01**), each block kept to a low level of detail. I tried to make these look unique from every angle, and then rotated and instanced them throughout the scene – although they were mainly kept in the foreground area where they would be better seen. Using instance over copy is ideal in scenes like this; the render engine can handle many more objects when they are instanced. (The total poly count for this scene was just over 5 million.)

Fig.01

FOG PASS

Fig.02a

Textures for the scene were very basic; there are perhaps only two or three major textures used. I wanted a very consistent look, as though everything had been made from the same surface types, with only the odd variation. The textures are each 2K in size, but because I used the 3d Studio Max bitmap pager I was only ever rendering them at half size.

Z-Depth Pass

Fig.02b

Lighting & Rendering

I have used finalRender for pretty much all my renders lately; I find it very easy and intuitive to work with. More importantly, it's very fast at rendering. I have a small affair going with the Maxwell renderer, but she takes so long to cook! For now, finalRender serves me well. My PC is a quad core with 2GB memory (32-bit). The quad core really helps at render time as each core adds another render bucket.

My render settings were kept as low as possible without losing too much quality. I used AQMC for the GI solution and Mitchell filtering; AA was set to Min.4/Max.16 samples. Rendering at 3500x1797, this shot took about four hours to render, which included several render elements – all the usual suspects: shadow, beauty, specular, GI, AO, fog, ZDepth (**Fig.02a – b**), etc.

For this image I used the physical sky lighting option in finalRender, which offers an accurate exterior lighting creation based on the Earth's position and the time of day. In max I overrode the earth setting with a compass helper, which helped in placing shadows correctly. This was an important step as the volume light was coming from a specific direction,

SOURCE: CGTEXTURES.COM

Fig.03

SCI-FI

which meant I had to match that direction in the physical sky. My material was also fairly basic; I was more concerned with specular and bump mapping as I knew these would play a large role in post-production. The volume light itself comes from a direct light placed behind the towers in the distance.

POST-PRODUCTION

This is where it all comes together and is the part I enjoy the most in the whole process – pulling all those rendered layers into Photoshop and having some fun! Starting at the back of the image I used a sky photo which was sourced from cgtextures.com (**Fig.03**); although you can barely see it in the final shot, it was a good idea to have it there as a starting point.

Fig.04

On a new layer set, I started adding in lighting details (**Fig.04**). These are usually just loose and quick brushstrokes, sometimes with overlaid photos of building windows at night – getting some building lights through the city helped to bring it to life. Another trick was to repeat lights off into the distance, which helped sell the depth of the image. All these "lights" were then blended using the Screen mode.

The specular element rendered in 3d Studio Max played a strong part in this image (**Fig.05**). You can see how the direct light creates a great wash of light across the building tops. As with the lighting layers, this was also "screened" above everything else.

Fig.05

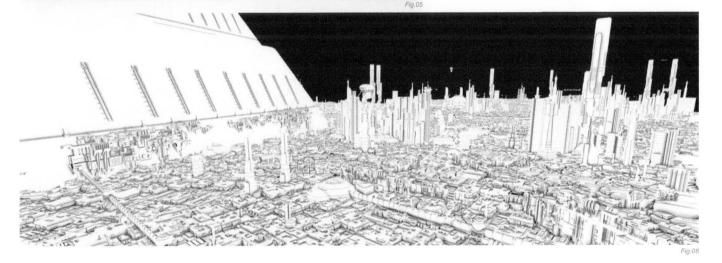

Fig.06

Fig.07

Another rendered element from 3d Studio Max was ambient occlusion (**Fig.06**). finalRender has a great feature called "detail detection", where the render rays are focused in areas where the mesh is connecting or intersecting. Playing with this setting I got some awesome detail that would otherwise not be visible. I also painted in some God rays at this stage (**Fig.07**). You can see most of the adjustments I made to the image in post-production, when compared with the raw untouched beauty render from Max (**Fig.08a – b**).

My Photoshop file tends to get fairly bloated after all this work, so collapsing layers wherever possible is important. I often collapse everything to a single layer and perform color correction, levels and curves adjustments. Finally, a touch of sharpening and the image was finished.

CONCLUSION

After finishing the still image I went to work on animating the scene. An animation can be seen online at www.stefan-morrell.com/goldlightfin2.mov. I used all the same techniques in creating the animation, except for using After Effects in place of Photoshop. All in all, a fun image to work on, and I'm sure I'll do more of these in the future.

Fig.08a

Fig.08b

ARTIST PORTFOLIO

THOM YORKE CARICATURE
BY ANDREW HICKINBOTTOM

SOFTWARE USED: 3d Studio Max, Mental Ray and Photoshop

INTRODUCTION

A creative and humorous forum (which I am a member of) holds fun weekly Photoshop challenges based upon current events/celebrities/ spoofs and so on. One week it was "Photoshop Thom Yorke". I thought I'd have a go in 3D, as I've always admired and wanted to try caricature art. Also keeping in with the "quick and dirty" spirit of the forum, I wanted to try and create it as quickly as I could.

After collecting reference photos of Thom Yorke (Radiohead's lead singer), as well as painted caricatures of him by different artists and references of caricatures in general, I began. I thought I would try to make a moodier, richer image than my usual bright, simplified, cartoony style. The image challenge on the forum changes every week, so I had a definite time window in which to do it – I couldn't afford to fine tune and obsess about all the little details like I normally would on a personal project.

WORKFLOW

Starting off with a box, I split it in half and used the symmetry modifier to speed things up. By using the connect tool to add edgeloops, the cut tool to add edges where needed, and good old fashioned vertex moving, I made the cube into a very simplified head shape, with the beginnings of the edgeloop structure for the mouth and eyes, as well as establishing a jaw line (**Fig.01** shows the initial modeling process). It's always important to get these fundamental things right early on as they can make adding detail a real pain if done wrong!

Using the same techniques, I continued to develop the head, adding detail and curvature. I had no definitive picture in mind for what this should look like. I nearly always design things as I model them because I get frustrated when trying to draw my ideas. I find it more productive to gradually alter and tweak the model until it looks right and matches the design in your head.

I made a start on the ears and hair and added basic eyes. It's best to roughly block out the main areas of your model as you go – I find it much easier to see it take shape this way. Continuing with the detailing, I spent a while establishing the size, position and shape of the

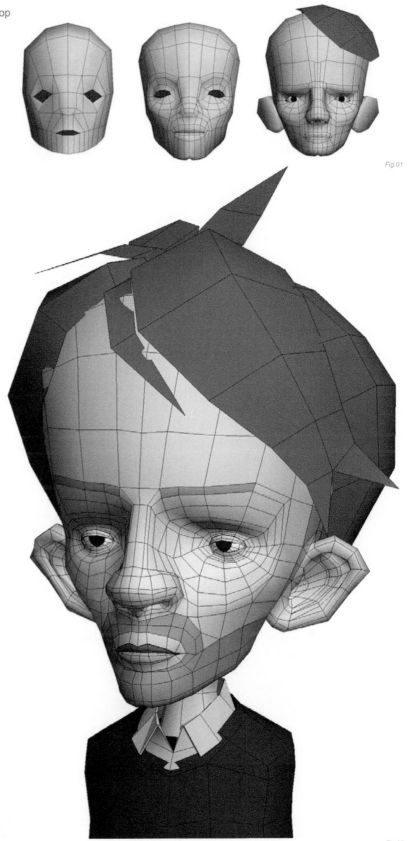

Fig.01

Fig.02

defining features. Looking at caricature art in general help to see what features are amplified or made smaller, whilst maintaining a likeness.

The polygons forming his stubble, brows and lips were colored to help visualize the end result. His body was blocked out from a box and an extruded plane with the shell modifier used to form his collar. I "grew" the hair using several edge extrusions of a plane and lots of vertex adjustments (**Fig.02** shows further modeling progression).

I added meshsmooth, completed his hair, then projected and unwrapped the UVs. The face texture is a Photoshop jigsaw of various parts of a high-res photo of Thom, combined with painted and cloned areas. The hair is simply blurred noise with the motion blur filter applied (**Fig.03** shows the head texture map and UV guides).

Due to the bright, simple and cartoony nature of much of my work, I have never really experimented with Mental Ray or final gathering. Given the short turnaround of

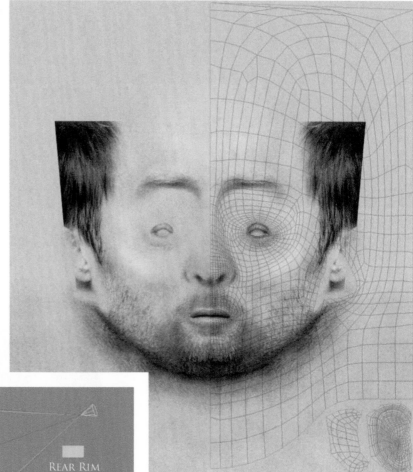
Fig.03

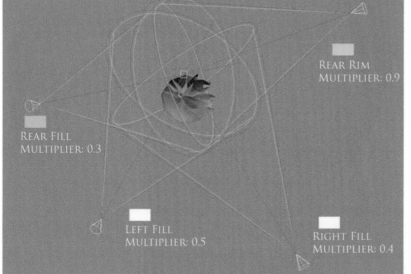

REAR RIM
MULTIPLIER: 0.9

REAR FILL
MULTIPLIER: 0.3

LEFT FILL
MULTIPLIER: 0.5

RIGHT FILL
MULTIPLIER: 0.4

Fig.04a

this image and its somewhat hurried construction, I thought I would do a quick experiment with Mental Ray's features as a small learning exercise. I added an SSS fast skin material for the subsurface scattering effect, and applied the texture and bump map. The lighting setup was relatively simple: four spot lights surrounding the model were adjusted to balance the light and dark areas on Thom's face. **Fig.04a** shows the position, color and intensity of the lights in the scene. It helped to isolate each light and see its effects on the scene before combining them. **Fig.04b** shows the light each of

REAR FILL   REAR RIM   LEFT FILL   RIGHT FILL

Fig.04b

the four spot lights produced when isolated. After much fine-tuning of the light settings and materials, I experimented with final gathering to bounce the light around in a more convincing way. A subtle three-step gradient material was added to the background. (**Fig.05a – b** shows the head shader with and without the textures.)

Next, I completed detailing and texturing on his body. Once completely satisfied with the look of the textured symmetrical face, I collapsed the modifier stack and worked on the asymmetry, such as his lazy eye, and skewing his jaw, ear and mouth a bit. Asymmetry makes a much more interesting caricature, and Thom has a few asymmetrical features – mainly his distinctive lazy eye.

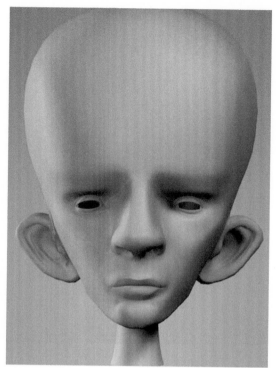

Fig.05a

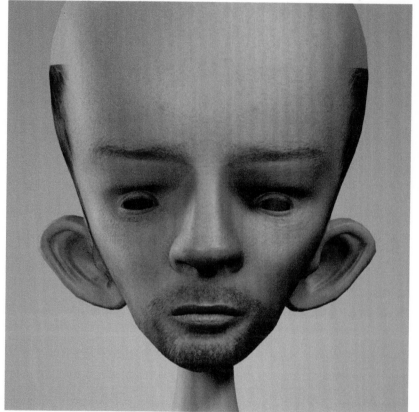

Fig.05b

I thought that the image was still looking a little too smooth, and the textured stubble sourced from the photo of Thom looked too flat. I added some hair to his face using Max's hair & fur tool. Using the styling tools and growth options, as well as a mask map to control coverage, I created his stubble and eyebrows. I tend to find procedurally generated hair doesn't "sit" on finished renders too well, so once happy with the look the hair was converted to geometry for ease of rendering. (**Fig 06a** shows the final unsubdivided model with the asymmetrical features; **Fig.06b** shows the final untextured model with asymmetrical features; **Fig.06c** shows its wireframe.)

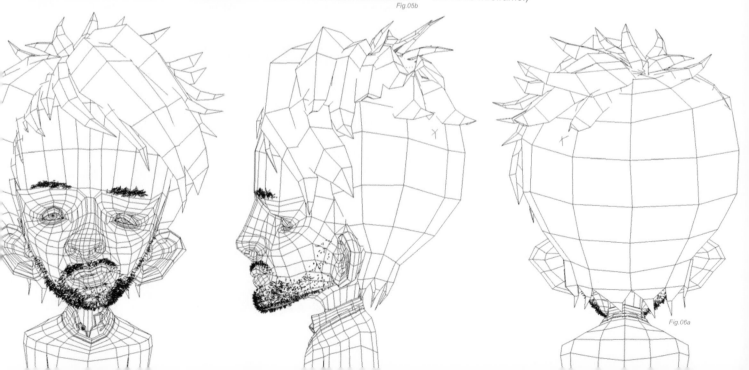

Fig.06a

Fig.06b

POST-PRODUCTION

I rendered an ambient occlusion pass to darken the shadows and add depth to his stubble. The levels, saturation and color balance were tweaked in Photoshop to give the right mood and make the image look a little richer and less "CG". I boosted the eye specular and "bloomed" the whole image slightly. The corners of the image were darkened and blurred to get a natural, out-of-focus vignette effect. (**Fig.07a** shows the ambient occlusion pass; **Fig.07b** shows the raw, unprocessed render; **Fig.07c** shows the layer processes in Photoshop used to create the final image.)

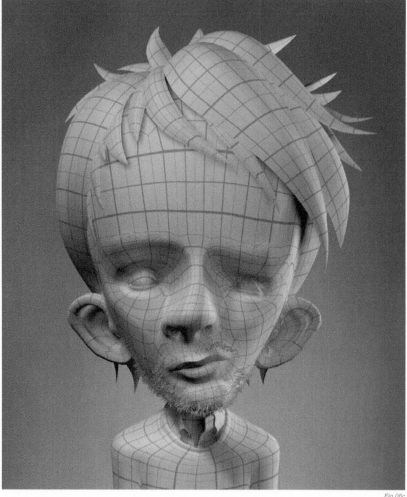
Fig.06c

CONCLUSION

Thom was made in unusual circumstances for me. He was a test to see if I could create something different in the form of a caricature, using a renderer and shaders I am not familiar with (and still don't fully understand) within a short timescale. The assertive, "don't think, just do" style of modeling was very rewarding when I saw how quickly he was completed. I am pleased with the end result, and feel like I have accomplished something by using Mental Ray to my advantage, and by creating my first caricature.

Fig.07a

Fig.07b

Fig.07c

THE UGLY DUCKLING
BY DENIS C. FELIZ

SOFTWARE USED: Photoshop CS3

INTRODUCTION

Before I became an artist with an academic qualification, I was an artist of a very intuitive and emotional manner; I used to represent things in a free and uncommitted way. Throughout my academic life I've learned a lot about techniques and other ways to represent things correctly. After finishing college I discovered that my drawing style had become quite strict – it was not so free anymore. Because of this, I couldn't work; I kept thinking about rules, proportion, tools, correct forms of graphic representation … I'm not saying that academic methods are wrong. Quite the opposite: they are really useful. However, in my case during this period of my life, I couldn't combine the sophisticated techniques I'd learned with my emotion and particular style of representation.

Fig.01a

CARTOON

This image, *The Ugly Duckling*, is one image of a larger study I'm currently working on; I'm trying to use a good drawing and painting technique, but in a way that expresses my personal style and feelings.

WORKFLOW

In the creative process I follow, for both 2D and 3D images, I give absolute priority to research and observation, because it's extremely important to know – in detail – what it is that you want to represent. I tend to search for ideas about things that have happened in my life, or in stories I have read. In the case of *The Ugly Duckling*, I was inspired by the story by Hans Christian Anderson: the fairytale of a swan egg that is accidentally put in a duck's nest.

After researching the concept, an image was almost complete in my head; just a few sketches were necessary in order to define the initial form that was to be painted. With this painting specifically, I wanted to represent an image that was obviously ugly, but also with an element of cuteness at the same time (**Fig.01a – b**).

What I found really interesting was the duck's eyes. They are very asymmetrical, but they stay well located in the character's head, and neither the beak nor the general structure of the model is distorted by them.

Some things that I think are valuable in an image are the little details, so in this image I'm speaking of elements like the hair, feathers, veins, and a variety of tiny flowers that compose the scene. I was able to represent these details well because of the research that preceded the creation of the image, and I'm reiterating this here

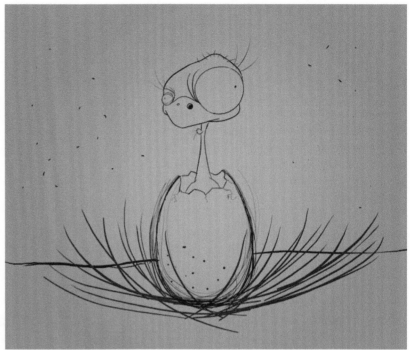

Fig.01b

Fig.02

Fig.03a

because I really think that the research step of the creative process is so very important. One challenge I came across was in painting an image with no outline, and by that I mean an image composed of only light and shadow to build the volume. A good tip for achieving a clean result around your drawing is to use the Pen tool in Photoshop to establish the base on which to paint (**Fig.02**).

Another important tip for anyone who wants to start in digital art is to not let discouragement and laziness make you stop painting. Give commitment to each part of the image and understand that the details are the main part of the scene. The result is a rich composition that viewers will spend more time looking at and appreciating.

Two things that I really respect in an artist, and that I try to do in my own productions, are 1) to escape from stereotypes, and 2) to participate in different areas of visual creation. I believe that I'm a versatile artist simply because I work with digital painting, 3D, photography and traditional art, and the most important thing I find is that I can combine all of these techniques together in just one image.

The results achieved in my illustration of *The Ugly Duckling* were very satisfactory (**Fig.03a – c**). Besides this being an image that for sure has my emotion built into it, my visual identity is also quite apparent and the painting technique respects some of the graphic production standards I learned at college.

FINAL THOUGHTS

With each day that passes, and each image I create, I develop a better visual perception through my research, which I am accumulating for future productions. This is why I keep looking at my old images so I can see areas where I can improve. One thing I always do, and I advise other artists to do as well, is to show their images to other artists to get information from those who have different outlooks. An excellent way to do this and to get quick replies is to submit your work to the various discussion

Fig.03b

forums online. I've grown up talking about my images a lot, as well as discussing images by other artists. Without a doubt, it's very effective.

Looking at *The Ugly Duckling* now and thinking about past conversations I had in online forums about it, I do believe that I could have done some things differently, for example the reflection in the character's eyes. I think I'd also add volume to all the grass leaves in the nest, and I'd create a secondary character, an insect, to complete and enrich the general composition of the image.

Fig.03c

© FABRICIO MORA

DON QUIXOTE DE LA MANCHA
BY FABRICIO MORAES

SOFTWARE USED: 3d Studio Max, Mudbox and Photoshop

INTRODUCTION

Don Quixote is a well known character, created by Miguel de Cervantes Saavedra, and has been represented by many artists throughout the centuries. One day I saw a statue of Don Quixote and, since I'd never seen a CG representation of it at the time, I decided to give it a try. I had no concept art whatsoever; I was inspired simply by an antique Spanish statue with very strong lines in its form, and I used photographs and old paintings that I found on the internet as some references for the project.

MODELING

For the modeling I used the "poly by poly" technique. It is a well-known technique and there are lots of tutorials

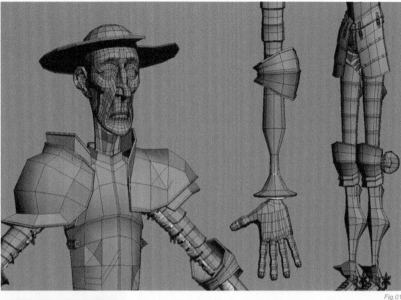

Fig.01

about this method, so I'm just going to show you the wireframes of the final model here – the entire model was built poly by poly (**Fig.01**).

With the model almost finished, I created a very simple rig to pose my character. I was then almost ready to export the model into Mudbox in order to add more details, like the wrinkles and skin folds. I also enhanced the bone structure a little. Before exporting to Mudbox from 3d Studio Max, I UVW unwrapped all of the models because the software keeps the mapping information of the original mesh, and I knew that I wanted to import the high poly model back into 3d Studio Max from Mudbox later on. It's a lot easier to unwrap a low poly model than the final mesh! So once I'd finished refining the model in Mudbox, I imported it back into 3d Studio Max, as planned (**Fig.02**).

All parts of the model were unwrapped separately, and almost all of them have a unique texture. For the armor

Fig.02

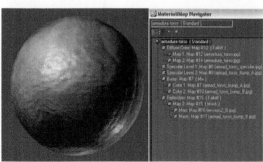

Fig.03

I used the same material setup but changed the maps slightly. My starting point was the torso, for which I used the setup shown in **Fig.03**; some of the maps used to texture it can be seen in **Fig.04**.

For the skin shader I used the following parameters (**Fig.05**); the maps for the skin are shown in **Fig.06**.

HAIR

I used 3d Studio Max's native Hair and Fur for the hair. I duplicated the head mesh and deleted some faces in order to isolate a small portion of the skull which would be used as the emitter for the hair. I then used Vertex Paint to paint out a mask that would tell the software where the thin hair would "grow" (**Fig.07**).

Not to slow down my render too much, I did the hair in a separate Max file and rendered it using the default

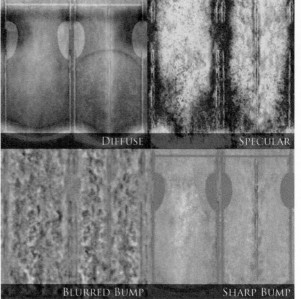

DIFFUSE SPECULAR

BLURRED BUMP SHARP BUMP

Fig.04 *Fig.05*

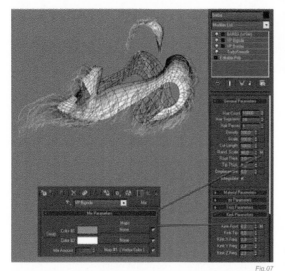

Fig.07

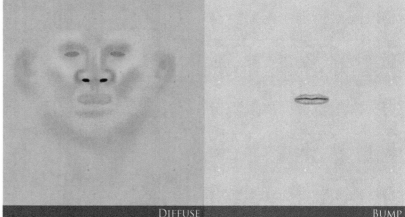

DIFFUSE BUMP

Fig.06

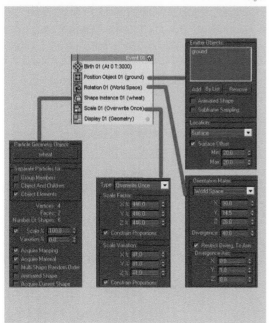

Fig.10

Fig.08 *Fig.09*

Scanline renderer. In order to make a perfect match between the Mental Ray rendered body and my Scanline rendered hair for post-production, I merged the final head mesh to the hair file and used the Matte/Shadow material. This way the hair strands occluded by the head shape wouldn't be rendered.

CREATING THE FIELD OF WHEAT

I actually have an easy solution for the making of the wheat field. If I tried to make it with geometry it would take ages to render – if it would render at all – so I decided to make it with a mapped plane mesh distributed by Particle Flow. The only problem with this was going to be the shadows in between, so I had to simulate them on the map itself. It wasn't the most accurate solution but it worked out just fine in the end. **Fig.08** shows the final wheat model.

I rendered six different branches of wheat and manipulated them in Photoshop to add more volume and to vary their color and tones a little. I then used the maps on planes

Fig.11

in 3D with their corresponding alpha in the opacity slot (**Fig.09**). I've shown the Particle Flow setup I used in **Fig.10**. The wheat had to be rendered using the Scanline renderer. The raw render ended up with less volume than I wanted but it was good enough for post-production (**Fig.11**).

LIGHTING & RENDERING

I used a mr Area Spot with raytraced shadows for the main light. One mr Area Spot was used for the back light with a shadow map and far attenuation, set to the shield's distance; one Omni was used for specular and a sky light was added for global illumination (**Fig.12**). You can see Mental Ray's Final Gathering configuration in **Fig.13**.

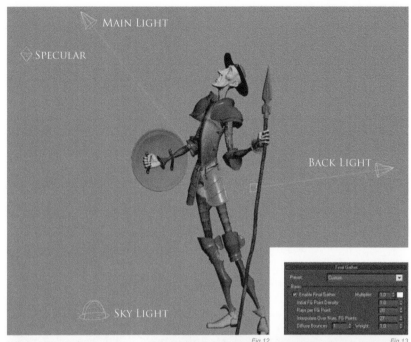

Fig.12

Fig.13

Fig.14b

Fig.14c

Fig.14a

POST-PRODUCTION

Here are the final render passes (**Fig.14a – e**). For the background plate I started painting gradients and mixed them with wall textures in Photoshop; using the windmill's alpha channel I made the shadows and defined the location of the horizon line (**Fig.15**).

I then set the windmill layer as an Overlay layer in order to mix it with the background and to achieve the same mood as illustrated in the rest of the composition. Using a new layer I enhanced the sun, simulating a stronger volume light. For the sky I mixed some different sky photographs from my library and applied a mask to it (**Fig.16**). For the layer of wheat I used the same Overlay blending mode that I used for the windmill. I then duplicated the layer and manipulated it to reach the idea of a larger field.

Fig.14d

Fig.14e

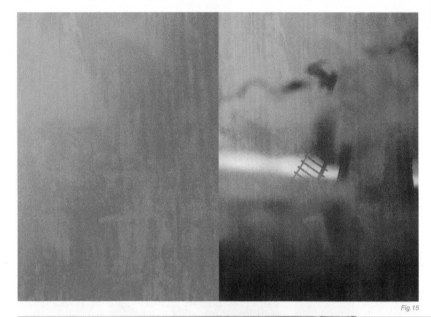

Fig.15

Before I could finally start color adjusting Don Quixote, I had to fix some minor render and texture errors. I usually ignore these kinds of errors prior to this stage because they're easily corrected here in Photoshop (if I was making an animation then I most certainly would have had to polish these things up earlier in 3d Studio Max).

Finally, with the color as I wanted it, I set the occlusion pass on top of everything with its blending mode set to Multiply. This helped to settle things down and also emphasized the contact shadows.

Fig.16

CARTOON

The beard was manipulated separately, as you can see in **Fig.17**. Final retouches were then made to increase the contrast in the whole composition, to bloom the lighting effect and to increase the highlights on the field of wheat some more (**Fig.18**).

CONCLUSION

It was very satisfying to see the final image and to realize that it had turned out exactly the way I had imagined right at the very beginning of the project. It was also interesting to use classical paintings as references for this project, to study them and to achieve a much better understanding of lighting and composition from doing so.

Throughout my research I discovered many representations of this fantastic character, from so many different artists – all with unique visions. I now feel as though I have become part of this, through the creation of my own vision of Don Quixote.

Fig.17

Fig.18

ARTIST PORTFOLIO

RAJUN' CAJUN' JUG BAND
BY GREGORY CALLAHAN

SOFTWARE USED: ZBrush

INTRODUCTION

Rajun' Cajun' Jug Band started from a sketch I did of an old hillbilly gold miner. My original idea was to sculpt an old gold miner striking gold, eyeing his golden nugget, but as I was blocking him out a friend of mine mentioned that he looked like a hillbilly and that he should be holding a banjo rather than a gold nugget. I continued to pursue my original idea, but after hearing his suggestion all I could see was this hillbilly with a banjo ... so I went with it! After completing the old hillbilly playing the banjo I didn't want to stop, so I set out to design more characters thus making up the *Rajun' Cajun' Jug Band*.

COMPOSITION & STYLE

Once I'd decided I wanted to make a band of characters, the main focus became the overall composition. I really wanted to make the characters look as if they were all playing to the same tune and interacting with each other. Since Pappy (the old hillbilly) was the first character I designed, he really set the tune for the rest of the

Fig.01

band (no pun intended). Shapes played a big part in the composition. I wanted each character to have a very distinct silhouette: Pappy being tall and skinny, Uncle Bob big and round, Bobby Sue being curvy, and so on. Another element I really wanted to add was animals and critters. They add great contrast to the human characters and no classic cartoon is complete without animals that can walk on two legs – the gator being the Cajun' equivalent to the watch dog, and the crawdad a Cajun' favorite finger food.

CARTOON

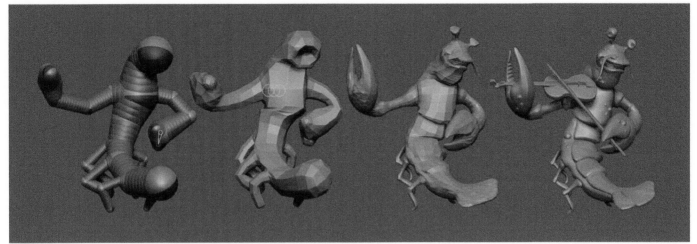

Fig.02

The basic style for this project was influenced by childhood memories of classic Warner Bros. cartoons. Having grown up watching countless hours of Chuck Jones and Tex Avery cartoons, my style has always borrowed something from the classic 2D animation masters. Knowing this, I made a point not to reference any classic cartoon characters in this piece. Instead, I used photos of unique people and made characterizations based on memories of some of my favorite childhood cartoons. I also did quite a lot of research on jug bands and found that there are a few basic instruments needed to complete the band: a banjo (Pappy), washboard (Uncle Bob), washtub base (Granny) and of course a Jug (Little Bobby Joe). Each character was designed around the instrument they play.

WORKFLOW

The initial execution of this project was not as smooth as I usually like it to be. I normally start off with a line drawing concept based on a combination of references I gather, and

Fig.03

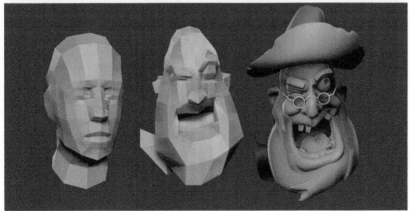

Fig.04

several other quick sketches I do to get my ideas down on paper. In this case, however, I tried to design both the characters and composition on the fly, since the idea evolved from one character. After finishing the first two characters – Pappy and Gator – I hit a stumbling block and could see this approach was not going to work. I then went back to the drawing board and sketched out a few compositions, as well as a quick color key (**Fig.01**).

From there I continued on with my basic pipeline that I use to create just about every character I do. For the most part I try to work in ZBrush as much as I possibly can. In this case, I would say 98% of it was completed in ZBrush, with the exception of using Photoshop for texturing and color correction. All base meshes for each character were created using a series of ZSpheres to rough in my basic pose. Once I was satisfied with the pose, I converted the mesh to a low-res mesh, which was then fine-tuned by adding additional geometry where more detail would be needed.

The mesh was divided into one to two more subdivisions and the Move tool was used to push and pull the geometry to help better define the character's silhouette. At this point, major features for the character were readable and represented the overall expression of the face, hands and body language. I would say this is the most important stage in the sculpting workflow. Much like a line drawing, if the model does not read well at this stage, all the details (wrinkles, textures, etc.) and colors added in the final stages are not going to help.

The last stage is by far my favorite – the details. This is where you can go crazy with all the minor details, like folds and wrinkles, and in this case the alligator skin, and so on. For the purposes of this piece I kept it somewhat simple. I wanted to stay true to the cartoon style and focus on major details, letting the viewer fill in

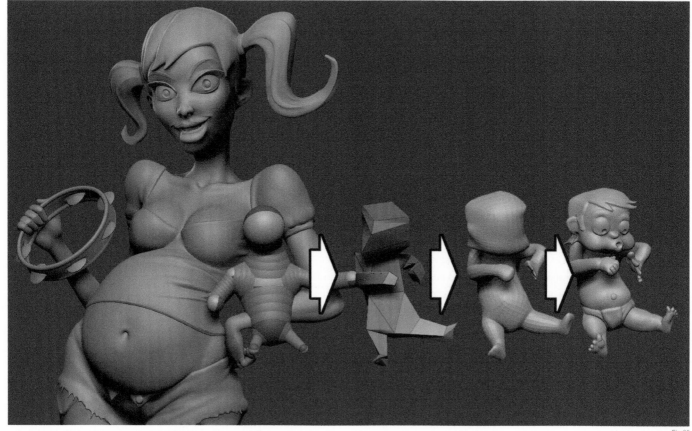

Fig.05

the blanks. **Fig.02** shows the steps described above as I blocked out the crawdad character to the final detail passes; **Fig.03** illustrates the work in progress stages of the alligator; **Fig.04** shows the sculpting progress of Pappy's head; and finally **Fig.05** illustrates the creation of Little Bobby Joe.

FINISHING TOUCHES
Once I was satisfied with all the character sculpts, I proceeded to texture each character. Again my approach was to keep it simple. The idea here was to not let the detail in the textures take away from the detail of the models, and so they were all hand painted using a combination of Photoshop and ZBrush. As you can see in **Fig.06**, the textures are basically a flat color with a dirt pass – nothing special. Less is more in

this case. The final render passes really pull it all together; as you can see, a combination of a flat diffuse, depth, rim light and specular render provide a polished final result.

CONCLUSION
One of the satisfying things about doing personal artwork is being your own art director and having the freedom to experiment with different concepts and techniques. With that being said, I had a blast making the *Rajun' Cajun' Jug Band*. It helped remind me why I love making characters so much. I find it enjoyable to create artwork in which the characters come to life. I like to think I create characters with character, and in this case people have told me they can practically see and hear this cast of characters – mission accomplished!

Fig.06

HOME SWEET HOME
BY IKER CORTÁZAR

SOFTWARE USED: Maya, Photoshop and Mental Ray

INTRODUCTION

At the time of this project I'd wanted for a long time to create some illustrations of exotic animals, living together with humans. One of the ideas I came up with was about a toucan. The initial concept was a toucan in a birdcage, poking his beak out through the gaps between the bars. My intention was to create a sad and slightly cruel story, but with a touch of black humor, because above everything else I wanted the image to be funny.

The toucan lives far from home; he can't move, he can only eat peanuts, and day after day he has to live with a kid that shoots arrows at him. His life couldn't be any crueler, but at the same time the situation is so ridiculous that I think it does actually become pretty funny. I like it when there's a background story to an image, but I don't like to show it too clearly – I prefer to suggest the story through the addition of details.

CONCEPT

I always start a project by searching for references; I believe that this is a very important step. I spent a lot of time searching the internet to find pictures of the

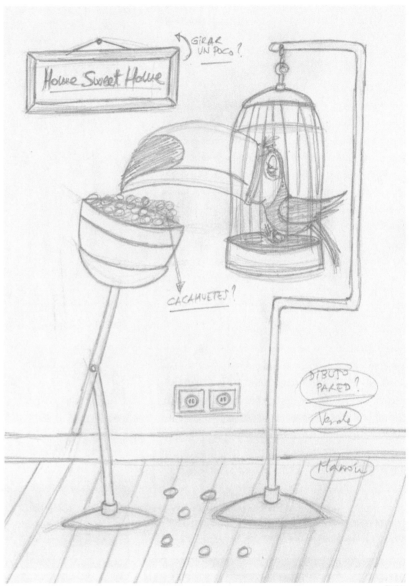

Fig.01a

Fig.01b

elements of the scene, especially pictures of toucans and birdcages. Once I had enough references, I started doing a sketch of the scene, which would help me to imagine the position of the camera and the composition of the image. I realized that the toucan was going to be the most important element of the scene, particularly his expression, so I did some more detailed sketches of the toucan for this reason (**Fig.01a – b**).

MODELING

The entire scene was modeled in Maya; I will try to explain how I modeled some of the objects. For the toucan's beak, for example, I created some curves following the shape of the beak in the sketch, and then used the Loft tool to get the surface (**Fig.02**). Other objects were modeled using the Revolve and Extrude tools – most of the elements of the birdcage were modeled this way, in fact. First I'd create the curves with the desired shape, and then I'd apply the Revolve or Extrude tool (**Fig.03**).

In other cases I began with primitive objects. For example, for the modeling of the peanut I began with a NURBS cylinder; I then closed the tips and gave shape to it by moving CVs. Finally, I used a bend deformer to give it its smooth curvature. Following that, I made several duplicates and gave those different sizes and curvatures (**Fig.04**). As well as this, I also used the box modeling technique to model a few of the other objects in the scene.

TEXTURING

Before texturing, I made several lighting and rendering tests to decide where to place the main light and to check how the scene was looking. I wanted the decor of the room to be slightly old fashioned – I thought that the retro atmosphere would make the situation even more ridiculous. I also liked playing with the idea of a brown floor and green wall, as if they were the earth and the vegetation of the toucan's natural home (**Fig.05**).

All the materials I used in the scene are Maya's own materials, except for the metallic material that I used for the birdcage and stand, which used one of Mental Ray's dgs_materials.

I used Photoshop to make the texture; in a few cases I started with a photograph and then painted onto it by hand, or I mixed it with some other files to achieve the desired texture. For the skirting board I started with a picture of a door frame that I took at home (**Fig.06**).

I also used an HDRI image – it was essential in order to improve the reflections of the materials (**Fig.07**).

LIGHTING

I didn't want there to be any windows in the room, as I thought this would make the toucan's life that little bit

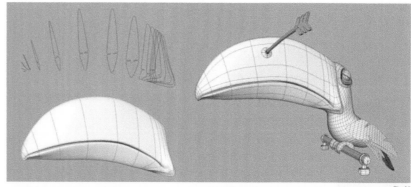
Fig.02

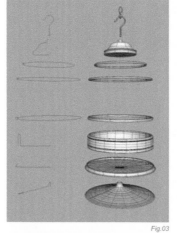
Fig.03

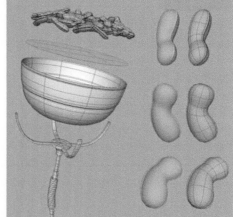
Fig.04

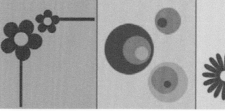
Fig.05

Fig.06

Fig.07

more claustrophobic. For lighting I therefore only used one spot light, which I placed on the ceiling as if there was a lamp flooding the room with artificial light (**Fig.08**).

In the Attribute editor of the light, I set Decay to Quadratic, converted it into a mental ray area light to soften the Raytrace shadows, and activated photons. I also used Global Illumination and Final Gather to light the scene.

The next step was to make several render tests, adjusting the Global Illumination and Final Gather settings. Once I got the desired result with the lighting, I adjusted the parameters of the materials. I also added two new spot lights to the scene, emitting only the specular. I connected one of them to the toucan's beak and the other one to the frame of the "Home Sweet Home" picture. I did this I order to emphasize those two elements a little (**Fig.08**).

RENDERING

Before doing the final render I corrected the orientation of the toucan's eye and the position of the eyelid to give him the expression I hoped for. I then rendered the scene with Mental Ray. The rendering was quite simple; I only rendered an occlusion pass besides the main RGB render.

POST-PRODUCTION

I used Photoshop for the post-production stage. During the render tests I realized that in some parts of the image it was very difficult to distinguish the edge of the birdcage because the metallic material was reflecting the wallpaper. I considered solving the problem with a back light, but I didn't want to add more lights to the scene … Instead, what I did was to render those parts of the birdcage again, but this time without reflections coming from the wallpaper. I then added those parts in Photoshop (**Fig.09**).

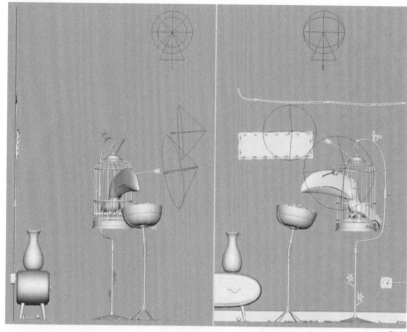

Fig.08

Fig.09

Fig.10

Finally, I made some contrast and brightness adjustments to the occlusion pass, and added it to the composited image (**Fig.10**).

CONCLUSION

Before considering any illustration finished, I always like to take another look at it after a few days' break, with fresh eyes, just to see how it looks from a new perspective. My intention with this image was to create a funny scene, in spite of the poor and pathetic life of the caged toucan. I can say that most of the people who have seen this image have found it somewhat amusing, so I feel happy with the end result and having achieved my original intentions.

ARTIST PORTFOLIO

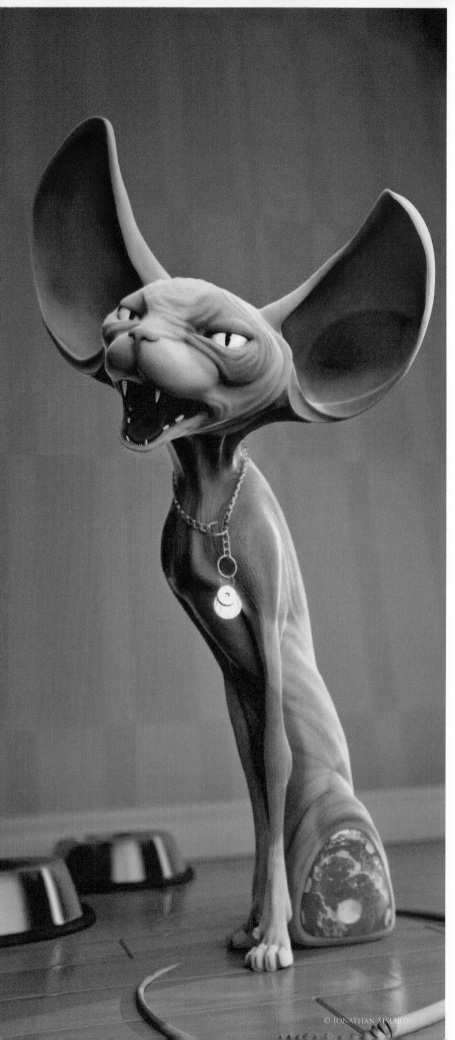

CLIVE OWEN
By Jonathan Simard

SOFTWARE USED: 3d Studio Max, ZBrush 3.1 and Photoshop CS2

INTRODUCTION

I'm not really a Clive Owen fan, but I named my picture this because my cat is named after the actor. I actually named my Clive Owen though because of an ongoing joke at work, and I'm sad to admit that this was my first inspiration. So with that said, let's begin with the interesting stuff!

WORKFLOW

For this picture I used a pipeline I experimented with during a picture I created before, called *White Teeth* (featured in *Digital Art Masters: Volume 2*). I found it worked really well for me, and so decided to continue using the workflow in a future project – Clive Owen was perfect for this. So throughout this article I will talk about my working pipeline, teach you some modeling tips and tricks (such as the awesome eye modeling technique!), and the process of color correction and compositing in Photoshop.

The basic idea was to use a 3D program of choice (which in my case was 3d Studio Max) simultaneously with ZBrush, and Photoshop with ZBrush. I didn't make any sketches or concepts for this image; I just knew that I wanted to model a sphinx cat cut in half. So the first thing I did was to find references. I took a week to search for references and then kept the best ones only for the project.

TIPS & TRICKS

Let's begin the fun with a few little tips I've developed about modeling an eye (**Fig.01a**). This particular eye modeling technique is something I developed because I was tired of losing time modeling eyes with the techniques I used to find in tutorials online. So here we go:

1. First of all, just add an eyeball (**1.1**). Pretty easy!
2. Add the tube and keep just the top (**1.2**) (the number of edges around the eye depends on you)
3. Align your tube to your sphere in translation with your sphere (**1.3**)
4. Align the interior hole of the tube to the surface of the sphere (**1.4**)
5. It is time now to make the first part of the eyelid (**1.5**)

6. And now the tricky part! The whole idea of this is to make the shape of your eye just using rotation – no more translation. No more! Yes that's right, and it'll work great! It does for me. What you have to do is select the tube and change its reference coordinate system (**Fig.01a**). Choose Pick and then select the sphere. Press and hold the button next to the reference coordinate system and choose the last one – Transform Coordinate Center (**Fig.01b**). Now select any vertex of your eye and the pivot will be at the center of the sphere. The beauty of it is that if you respect step 4, you just have to rotate any point and it will follow the shape of the sphere and you can easily make a great looking shape (**1.6**).

I always work with a low poly shape of the whole model. I don't need to add detail; I just need to be sure of the base model before doing any work in ZBrush. When the base model is done in Max (**Fig.02**), I then export my model into ZBrush. In ZBrush I don't add any subdivisions at first, I just re-work my shape with the Move tool until I find

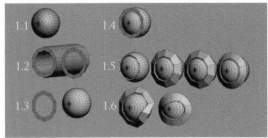

Fig.01a

REFERENCE COORDINATE SYSTEM

TRANSFORM COORDINATE CENTER

Fig.01b

something cool, after which I export it back into Max. This way I can sculpt my character more easily. Back in Max I can then add more subdivisions and change the pose as I wish. I go through a process of working between ZBrush and Max, re-importing to ZBrush and working again with the Move tool, then re-exporting to Max. I do a lot of importing and exporting of my models between Max and ZBrush without adding any subdivisions (I just add a little in Max if I need to). I'm just sculpting it (**Fig.03**).

Once I am finished in Max and my UVs are also done, I add a smooth modifier with an iteration of 1, and re-export the model back into ZBrush. This is a crucial step because you have to add more subdivisions before exporting anything to ZBrush – add more polygons where there are not enough subdivisions because your model needs to have polygons of approximately the same size around the model. This way you will have the same amount of detail everywhere in your model. It's a lot better to add plenty of subdivisions in a single area in Max rather than adding another level of subdivision in ZBrush for the sake of one area in particular.

I tried to keep the poly count around 400K when all the ZBrush detail was added to this model (**Fig.04**). I then exported it back into Max. Sure, I could have used a displacement map instead, but I'm never satisfied with it and I simply prefer to have the whole ZBrush model in Max.

So with the modeling all finished, it was time for the texturing. I won't talk about what brushes I used, because I'm not a good texture artist, but I will talk about the overall process in general. First of all, I started all my textures in ZBrush. I never start something directly in Photoshop because it's hard to judge if you're adding

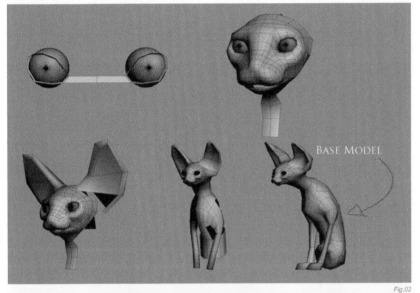

BASE MODEL

Fig.02

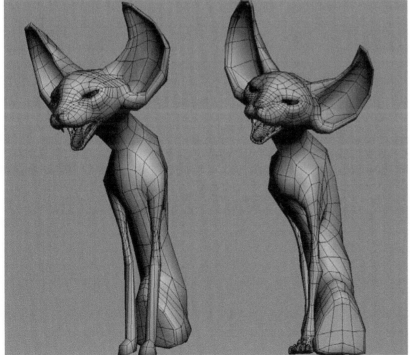

Fig.03

detail in the right places. For this image, texturing the large colored circles would have been impossible in Photoshop! It was really easy though in ZBrush with the Projection Master; I just used a normal circle brush and I exported the texture back into Photoshop (**Fig.05**). You don't need to add color in ZBrush, because you can do all this in Photoshop after.

Once the textures were done and the image was rendered, it was time for the color correction. As you can see, the rendered version looks pretty crappy compared to the final (**Fig.06**). I went through many stages in post-production to achieve a better result in Photoshop – here are the important ones:

1. On the rendered image, try and play with the Auto Levels/Color/Contrast adjustment under Image Adjustments – it will often make your picture better

2. Copy your original picture and put it on top of all the layers, and change the blending mode. Personally I used a lot of Overlay and Soft Light layers in this piece. Also play with the opacity and the Hue/Saturation of the layer

3. Copy your original picture and put it on top of all the layers. Change the color for black and white and add a lot of contrast. Change the layer blending mode to Linear Dodge and it will accentuate all the specular in your image

4. You can then add several new layers of light and change the layer mode again for Linear Dodge. For this image I rendered a thin black and white falloff to get a rim light (**Fig.07**); the second example in **Fig.07** was a render with one light to give more contrast

5. You can play with the colors and try the different tools under Image Adjustments until you reach something that suits your personal tastes.

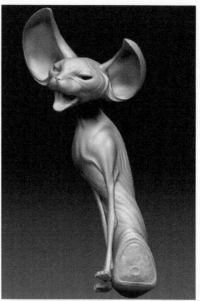

Fig.04

Fig.05

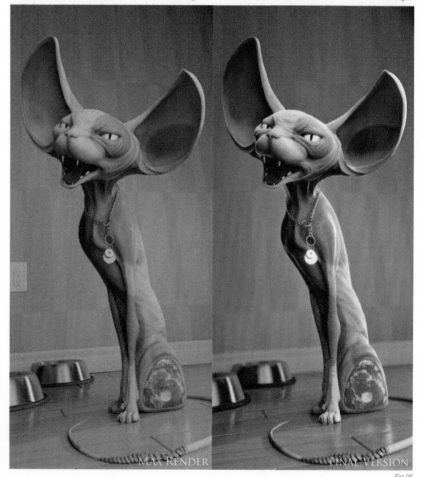

MAX RENDER

FINAL VERSION

Fig.06

CONCLUSION

During the process of every picture I have created, there have always been new things that I have learned. One thing I'd like to conclude this article with is a piece of advice: try to take risks and experiment with new things! The majority of the tips and tricks I have mentioned in this project overview are the result of a lot of trial and error – or just from chance. Try to go above tutorials and project overviews that you read, and you will discover new personal ways of working.

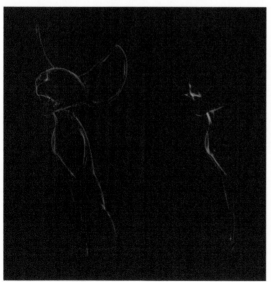

Fig.07

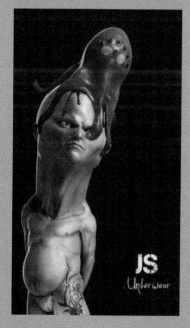

Munki
By Martin Carlsson

Software Used: 3d Studio Max and Photoshop

Introduction

Munki started out as an illustration I did while doing my internship at a local print and design company. Basically I was asked to do a picture of a funny monkey, maybe holding a banana. The image was never used, however, so the final picture was done at home, which meant I didn't really have any restrictions on how it should look. So, after taking the monkey home, my aim was to make an image of a simple, stylized and cute monkey, with some minor mental issues.

Getting Started

Since I hadn't modeled any monkeys before, the first thing I did was to collect some reference images to get a sense of the characteristics. As luck would have it, there are plenty of monkeys on the internet. Since it was supposed to look cute I based the

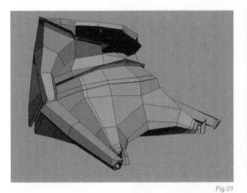

Fig.01

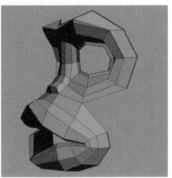

Fig.02

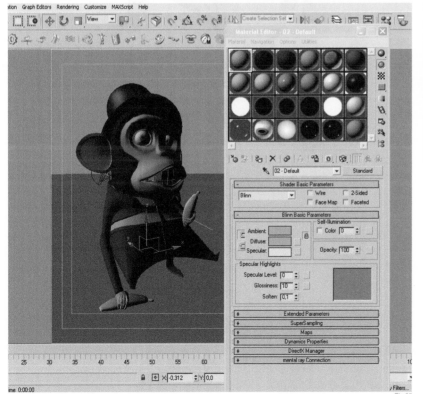

Fig.05

Fig.03

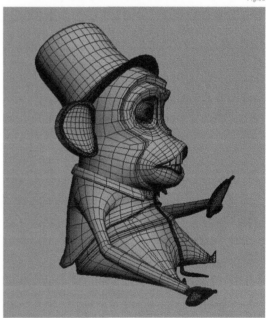

Fig.04

head on some nice pictures of a baby chimpanzee. I had a vague idea of how I wanted the body to look, basing it on my mental image of a proportionally challenged orangutan. I did not find any suitable references for that though.

Modeling in 3d Studio Max

When I had some solid references, I started blocking out the big shapes in 3d Studio Max (**Fig.01**). I didn't have a clear concept but chose to experiment on the model directly instead. For the body I began with a simple box and used the standard modeling tools, such as cut, connect, chamfer and extrude, to build up the shape. The head was modeled by extruding edges from the edgeloops around the eyes and mouth (**Fig.02**).

To save a bit of time when modeling, I use the keyboard shortcuts for switching between the vertex and, edge and face editing modes, as well as using the right-click menu to switch between tools. The same applied for move, rotate and scale. It's really worth spending some time learning the keyboard shortcuts, or even better setting up your own. It gives a nice flow to modeling and speeds it up considerably (**Fig.03 – 04**).

SETTING MATERIALS, LIGHTING & RENDERING

Since the aim was to make a simplified and stylized little monkey, I did not spend any time unwrapping the model or creating textures, except for the eyes. Instead I simply assigned differently colored standard materials by selecting the faces (**Fig.05**).

For the light I used Mental Ray and the daylight system with final gather turned on. It gives a rather nice light to work with later in Photoshop, for a minimum amount of work. I didn't care much about how the image looked at this point, as long as it had some niceness to it and the shadows and light fell in the right places. It was going to be severely altered in Photoshop later anyhow (**Fig.06**). To have more things to play around with in Photoshop, in

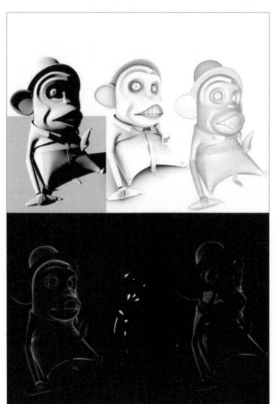

Fig.07

Fig.06

addition to the beauty pass, I rendered out six other passes consisting of one shadow, one ambient occlusion, two falloff and two specular passes (**Fig.07**).

POST-PRODUCTION IN PHOTOSHOP

Munki was always only ever going to be a still picture, thus I had total freedom to play around with it in Photoshop, which is a part I enjoy very much. Usually I start by simply throwing together the different passes in various blending modes (**Fig.08**) – I really enjoy scrolling through the blending modes. I almost always find some awesome color combination by changing things around here.

Next up I adjusted the colors, levels, saturation and opacity on the individual layers, possibly trying out some different blending modes again. I try to work as non-destructively as I can, using adjustment layers and layer masks on almost everything

(**Fig.09**). It's a really a nice and quick way of adjusting the look of the image. Instead of spending lots of time tweaking the materials and waiting for renders in 3d Studio Max, I rendered out a bunch of basic passes and simply masked the unwanted areas.

Once I was satisfied with the overall feeling of the composited image, I grouped the passes and their adjustment layers and started to make changes to the whole image. I added some textures to the background to give it a dirtier look, and then framed it with a vignette. I also did some major color adjustments to the whole picture, making it warmer overall. I finished the image by fixing some minor artifacts by painting over them.

CONCLUSION

This illustration was a great learning experience and I had lots of fun making it. There are of course things I wish I'd spent more time on, such as the shape of the hands and

Fig.08

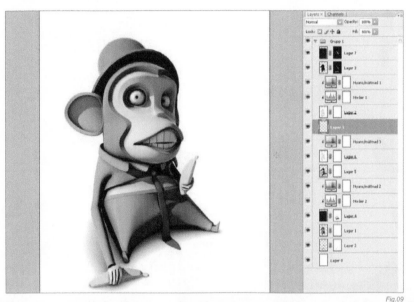

Fig.09

teeth which I find a little stiff. I also think I could have worked more with the lighting, punching it up a notch and making it a tad more dramatic. Overall though, I think I accomplished my goals with this image, and I'm pleased with the result. I hope you like it as well.

ARTIST PORTFOLIO

KIDS
By Michal Kwolek

SOFTWARE USED: 3d Studio Max, V-Ray, Photoshop CS3 and Unfold3D

CONCEPT

This particular piece was created for a contest on a Polish CG portal, max3d. pl. The subject was "The Terrible Consequences of TV Malfunction". My idea was to show a married couple who, due to a TV malfunction, found "other ways" of entertaining themselves: making babies. I wanted to show the kids playing up and causing their parents great annoyance, which was also the core of this terribleness. I wanted to create the whole image in a cartoonish, colorful style, so it could be easily readable and warm in its atmosphere and mood.

MODELING

I started the modeling process by creating the characters (**Fig.01**). I figured that I was going to need three models for the characters in my scene: a dad, a mum and a kid. There are five kids in the final composition, but it's the same model with slight differentiations, such as changes in the facial expression or haircut.

I used the poly modeling technique for the models, which gave me great control and ability. The overall shapes of the models were created from a single polygon; they are very simple models with a low polygon count (**Fig.02**), which employed smoothing (Turbosmooth) when necessary. Simple biped skinning was a good choice for setting up the poses for the characters as it was fast and simple (**Fig.03**).

I then modeled the couch, television set and the rest of the stuff in the scene. I sacrificed most of my time on the television (**Fig.04**); after all, it was meant to be the main

Fig.01

Fig.02

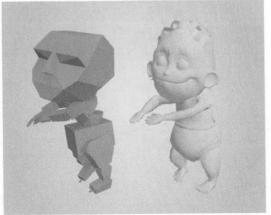

Fig.03

"character" in the scene! There are a lot of small pieces in it that are not even visible, and I gave it a decent amount of wires, cables and so on. These additional models were nothing more than lofted shapes along the splines. Most of them were created without any concepts, just modeled as I imagined them.

The room itself was made of two boxes connected by the doorway, which gave me a room and a kitchen. To create wallpaper which was coming off the wall, I just applied flat surfaces and modified the corners so they would look convincing enough.

Besides the handmade models I also used the cloth modifier. For the rug on the right of the scene I applied the modifier and simply "threw" it onto the ground. Thanks to that

CARTOON

I achieved a realistic shape and some nice folds in the cloth. Finally, the surface of dad's slippers and the carpet were both enhanced with the displace modifier and a procedural noise map.

TEXTURES & MATERIALS

The textures in this scene were very simple; in most cases created from scratch, but based on procedural textures (such as the wood elements, rug and blanket). The adults' and kids' clothing were just multiplied, simple patterns modified to fit the UV mapping applied. I had the most fun working with the pictures on the wall – especially the one from the wedding day. This photo was a mix of a wedding photo that I found with the heads of dad and mom overlaid on top. I had to do some over-painting work on the heads, but it was worth it (**Fig.05**). The rest of the pictures were created from renders and modified a little in 2D (color correction, composition, adding the background, etc.). The skins of the characters were painted with a simple brush in Photoshop – there's not much detail, but that was the look I was going for.

The materials used in this scene were basic VRay materials. Every single one had a diffuse channel and reflection with a falloff based Fresnel. Only the wallpaper material consists of two sub materials: the main and the embossed, shinier pattern.

LIGHTING

The key light in this scene was a warm light coming from the lamp; it's this lamp which illuminates the characters the most, as well as the room as a whole. This light is the one placed just above the lamp model and it was given a value of two. The shadows were area VRay shadows which gave them the desired softness. The next important light was the one from behind the window. To create this one I set up two direct lights with a soft, bluish tone, imitating the blue light of night and one white light to act as direct moonlight. The rest of the lights were Omni lights with the color set to blue that fill the right side of the room and the kitchen. There are also two

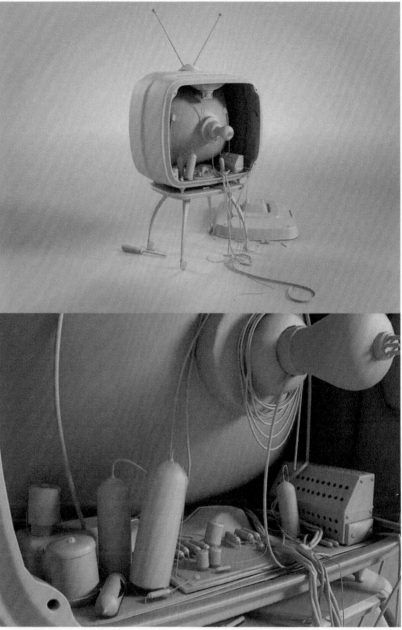

Fig.04

more lights giving additional illumination to the characters, set very closely to them and with very low values, like just 0.2 or 0.3. Every light has an option decay set to Inverse Square. This option gives a nice light fade effect the further away it is from the source. I recommend this because it allows you to get great lighting in a fairly simple way.

Fig.05

Fig.06

RENDERING & POST-PRODUCTION

I used V-Ray as my rendering engine, and the final image
was rendered in four passes: diffuse, reflection, color and
ambient with GI; the resolution of each was 4000x3000
pixels, and an antialiasing VRaySincFilter was also used
(value 4.0), which gave nice, balanced, sharp edges.

I didn't modify the rendering settings; I used defaults
(which is medium for the GI tab). It gave me a satisfying
effect with a fairly low rendering time. After compositing
the passes I then color corrected some areas. I didn't
want to "ruin" the original piece after the rendering
so I did the corrections on adjustment layers. These
layers don't influence the image directly and they're
created with a mask as you go, so this gives you a lot
of control overall. The image after color correction was
different from the one before, mainly with regards to the
contrast and saturation (**Fig.06 – 07**). I also modified the
characters' skin a little as well, adding a bit more life to it.

Fig.07

CONCLUSION

I think that I managed to get the right effect with this
image, and I actually won the contest for which this piece
was originally created! I'm most satisfied with the colors

and composition; the only thing that I'd change now is the number of kids. I think that
there should be some more of them, and also they seem a bit too good. They don't
appear to misbehave as much as I had wished. A lot of people also told me that dad's
pose is not very readable. Well, maybe that's the way it is? Dad ought to just look at a
hole in his sock and say, "Oh no, another problem!"

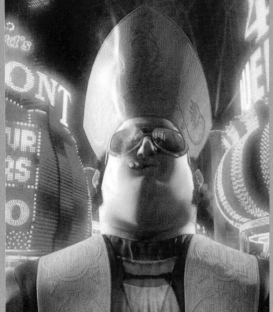

CAN'T SMILE WITHOUT YOU
BY TILL NOWAK

SOFTWARE USED: 3d Studio Max, V-Ray and Photoshop

INTRODUCTION

The image *Can't smile without you* is my second artwork about cute little animals, following *The Shaved Bumblebee*. Before that I used to produce science-fiction or design related works, but last year I discovered my obsession with designing funny little animals which are intended to look so ridiculous that you can't decide whether they are cute or just pitiful. My psychologist says this has something to do with the hamsters I loved as a child…

Anyway, regardless of my image topics, I always concentrate on strong geometric compositions, lighting and color scheme. In this case I tried to contrast the most ridiculous content with the very geometrical concept of using spheres everywhere. You can find at least 12 spheres in the image (**Fig.01**); it's like a "spherical world" – a tribute to this most basic and purest form of our universe. I had always been impressed by the power of spheres; good examples can be found in several designs of the movie *2001: A Space Odyssey*, as well as the federation ships in *Star Wars: Episode II – Attack of the Clones* and the works of the artist Erwin Wurm, who plays these geometrical games ingeniously! It somehow seems satisfying to consolidate complex natural shapes into more powerful basic shapes – or at least it's fun to do so!

MODELING

The project started with the idea of an exaggerated fugu fish. I never do sketches; I always start working

Fig.01

Fig.02

Fig.03

Fig.04

Fig.05

Fig.06

Fig.07

directly in the 3D software which I use as my kind of sketchbook. So from the idea I quickly modeled the fish in ZBrush (**Fig.02 – 03**) and let the scene rest for a few months. When I returned to it, I started thinking about a surrounding scene, and then created the cat (**Fig.04**).

The rendering was created in 3d Studio Max (**Fig.05 – 07**), but this was only half the work because I am very passionate about excessive 2D editing on top of raw 3D renderings (**Fig.08**). In just a few hours of good 2D editing you can boost the quality of some 3D work you may have spent weeks with, so I'm now going to focus on the following workflows which bring the depth and detail into my works.

COLOR SCHEME

One of the first and most important things I do after the 3D image is rendered is to define an overall color scheme (**Fig.09**). The goal is to create tension between warm and cold as well as light and dark parts. The cat and the fish divide the image into a warm and soft part, and a cool underwater part. I used a simple gradient in Photoshop and a mask to define which parts of the image were more

Fig.08

Fig.09

or less influenced by this layer. You can see the difference if you compare the paper lamps in the background. Having a strict color composition brings stability and depth into the image. Additionally, I added partial glows and lens flares to make lighter parts shinier (**Fig.10**).

MORE 2D ENHANCEMENTS

Sometimes, I tend to not even finish my 3D geometry because I already know I will fix it later in Photoshop. The face of the cat for example was modeled only roughly in 3D (**Fig.11**); I simply decided to paint the nose, hair and shadows over the basic 3D model. I did the same with the badly textured paw (**Fig.12**), using the fur-brushing workflow (which I will describe later). Another example is the texture of the fin (**Fig.13**), and the fish's face was also edited (**Fig.14**) – it was originally looking towards the cat, which seemed to be the logical action in its situation, but I consciously decided that the fish should not look at the cat; I liked it to appear more miserable this way, as if it already had got used to the situation and could see its fate as inevitable.

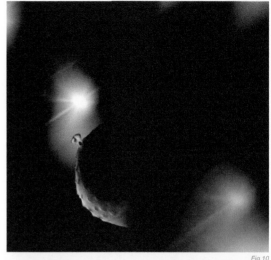

Fig.10

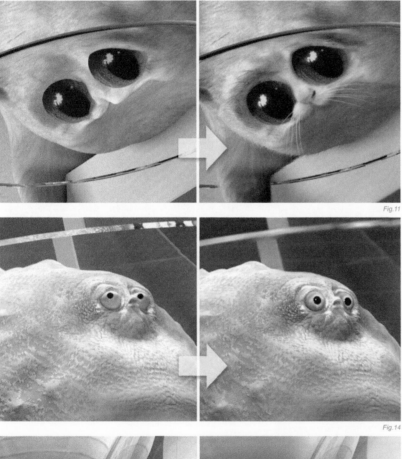

Fig.11

Fig.14

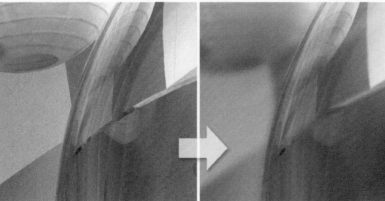

Fig.15

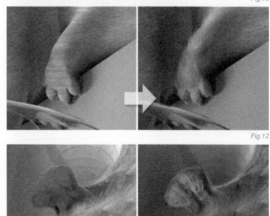

Fig.12

Fig.13

TO BLUR OR NOT TO BLUR?

If it was a real photograph there would be almost no depth blur, because it is a wide angle perspective which stays sharp regardless of the distance, due to optical rules. But luckily it isn't a real photo, so as an artist I am allowed to choose subjective modifications if it helps the overall composition (**Fig.15**). Adding depth blur is a good tool to strengthen the impression of perspective and to focus it on the important parts. And to make life easier it is also great for covering up less detailed parts.

PAINTING THE FUR

For me, the most interesting workflow in the editing process of this image was creating the fur in a quick and easy way (**Fig.16**). From my earlier experiences with fur tools I knew that I would usually need a long time to configure the hair, and it would still require a lot of editing and fixing afterwards. So I just wanted to come up with a much easier and faster solution, and finally solved it in Photoshop within 20 minutes, instead of the hours I would have spent with a 3D hair tool.

As a starting point I needed to texture the cat with a basic fur texture. I then used the Smudge tool in Photoshop to just smear the color of the textured object in thin curved lines over the edge and away from the object (**Fig.17**). Using the Fade option in the brush panel will give you a nice soft end of the line which results in the fluffy look. The number 200 will become the length of one hair in pixels. Adjust the Fade length and the size of the brush until it looks furry, depending on the image resolution you are working with.

OPTICAL DISTORTION

Basically a slightly curved line creates more tension than a straight line, so I sometimes use a little distortion

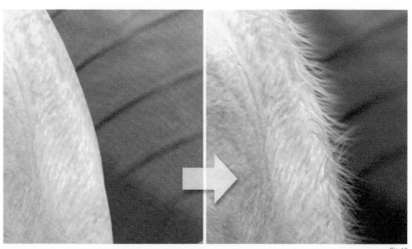

Fig.16

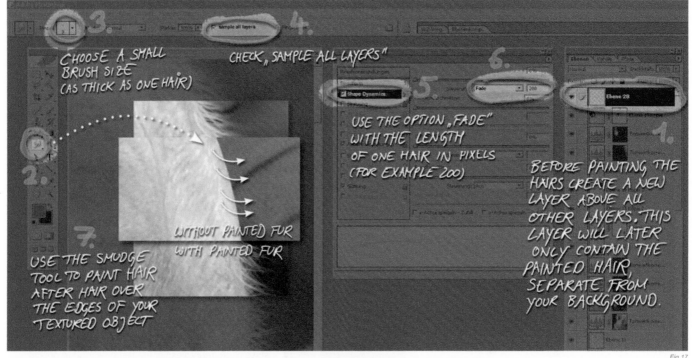

Fig.17

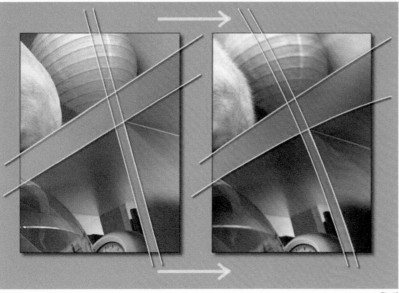

to bring more tension into the composition. In real photography a wide angle shot like this would be visibly distorted, but in a 3D rendering all straight lines stay straight unless you add the distortion manually (**Fig.18**). Not caring about scientific correctness I added the distortion only to the right part of the image to underline the glass bowl as the central spherical form.

CONCLUSION

Compared to my other works this image was not the most technically complex thing to create, but it continued what I had started with *The Shaved Bumblebee* – to tell a little story in one image and to combine it with a very graphical concept at the same time. This combination makes me happy, so I will continue creating ridiculously absurd animals like this. Or I might just get a real little hamster and become happy with it...

Fig.18

CARTOON

© Weiye Yin

FLY TOGETHER
BY WEIYE YIN

SOFTWARE USED: 3d Studio Max, DeepPaint 3D/BodyPaint 3D and Photoshop

INTRODUCTION

The inspiration for *Fly Together* came from an aged wooden toy; my original inspiration for making this image came from reminiscing about my childhood. Toys in my childhood were usually made of wood or sheet-iron; simple structures and bright colors. Compared with the modern toys of today that are varied and offer many methods of play, they were clumsy and of weak playability. Children therefore, at the time, often invented games by themselves, for example using puppets attached to string that they waved about, chasing one after another. Painted puppets became obsolete over time; playmates from childhood go in different directions and pursue their own dreams. This is what this particular artwork represents: they are flying, in different directions – still smiling, but with aged faces; only a line links them all; they seem to be free and happily chasing, but the concept also implies an element of constraint and helplessness.

THE SKETCH

As time has flown by, both puppets as objects and photo references of them have become difficult to find, and so I created a sketch for this project using just a blurry memory (**Fig.01**). To complete the design in 3D seemed fairly easy. The basic shape of the puppets is cubic, their

Fig.01

colors are simple, and their types are similar, so there is little technical content in the making of these little characters. However, because of the overly simple shape of these objects, it becomes very difficult for the work to attract the viewer's attention, so this had to be taken into consideration here.

So how do you attract the viewer's attention with such a simple concept? A successful work needs to consider many aspects, represent details, and bring together a common understanding within the audience. All of this requires much thought and investigation before starting the modeling of any design.

MODELING & TEXTURE DESIGN

Platform toys (or canvas toys), which are very popular at present, gave me plenty of inspiration for my puppet characters in this artwork. Platform toys are blank canvases

Fig.02

Fig.03

Fig.04

Fig.05

that incorporate patterns and designs of different topics on plain colored surfaces; they come in different types but their differences are created purely in the process of their coloring and in their patterned exteriors. A key characteristic of a platform toy is its simplicity, and it was this element that I wanted to bring into my own artwork and puppet designs.

To start things off in 3D, I began modeling according to my original sketch (**Fig.02**). To suit textures of different styles, the model had to remain as simple and neutral as possible, and I stayed aware of the fact that I was not to add any detail that would create any kind of "personality" in the model.

Moving on to unwrapping the UVs, according to the sketch the angle of view of the final render would show the major faces at the front. Faces other than the back and bottom (the green areas in **Fig.03**) should therefore have evenly spaced UVs (this method can only be used in static works). The reasonable layout of UVs was also helpful for when I came to change the texture designs afterwards.

I created the first base texture according to the UV layout (**Fig.04**), and I created the complete set of base textures for the other puppets in the same way (**Fig.05**). My texture designs were consistently simple with distinct personalities, using single colors for large areas. This was not only easier for the connection of patterns, but it was also easier to distinguish the characteristics of the different puppets.

Fig.06

I painted the effect of dropped, spilled paint onto a wooden texture to create an overlay layer for my base textures. Painted wooden surfaces will wear, and so I also painted some concentrated areas of stripped paint at the edges, emphasizing the worn edges and connections using DeepPaint 3D or BodyPaint 3D (**Fig.06**).

I overlaid the worn wooden texture with the puppet color map to create the final color map, to add further characteristics to my dated puppets (**Fig.07**). The final textures have both bright colors and worn details; the worn wooden textures could also be used as a bump map as well.

ATMOSPHERIC RENDERING & POST-PRODUCTION

Models and textures are the most basic elements of any static artwork. So how do you make a work full of vigor? Well the details of main objects alone are not enough, there should be corresponding atmosphere also.

To simulate the wide angle effect of a fish-eye lens, I arranged the puppets in their positions randomly, to create the feeling of them flying forwards at different angles and distances apart. The most forward puppet is the leading actor, and the other puppets are the supports and positioned according to this structure. Each puppet has its own color; the striking balance between the different blocks of color in the image makes the final render work.

Considering the downward angle of the models, I chose a photograph of a hallway with a semi-bird's eye view to act as my background for the image, upon which I painted a banister in the foreground. I then applied a Gaussian Blur in Photoshop to simulate depth of field, and as the leading puppet is pink colored, I tinted the background blue for better contrast.

CARTOON

I set the main light source according to the background image; to achieve consistent lighting and shadow effects, there had to be only one floodlight in the work. As the puppets are in mid air, I used Mental Ray to render the global lighting effect, and I supplemented this with a "sub-light". Through this, the indoor effect of rich lighting was achieved (**Fig.08**).

I added a small reflection value to the material, besides the color map and bump map, which would not influence the overall effect, but did increase the feeling of illuminated faces.

Fig.07

Lastly, I rendered the models layer by layer, and then took them into Photoshop for post-production work, where I added some blur for the depth of field effect (the further from the camera, the blurrier the puppets) to distinguish the hierarchy of the characters. I also add some Motion Blur beyond the zoom lens to increase a feeling of movement, and I added a halo to the light source, increasing the contrast and therefore allowing the overall image to become more vivid (**Fig.09**).

CONCLUSION

To attract the viewers' attention with such simple work, you need a novel design for the shape (and texture), skilful color co-ordination, rich colors and consistent atmospheric rendering. If these requirements are met, an even simpler object could be present in an interesting and successful work – rich and full of meaning.

Fig.08

Fig.09

ARTIST PORTFOLIO

THE 2009 DIGITAL ART MASTERS

ALEXEY
KASHPERSKY

kashperskya@gmail.com

http://arttalk.ru

http://rid.at.ua

ANDRÉE
WALLIN

andree.wallin@gmail.com

http://www.andreewallin.com

ANDREI
KASHKIN

xmyth1@gmail.com

http://xmyth.cgsociety.org/

ANDREW
HICKINBOTTOM

chunglist2@btinternet.com

http://andyh.cgsociety.org

ANDRIUS
BALCIUNAS

cryinghorn@gmail.com

http://www.cryinghorn.com

ANDRZEJ
SYKUT

azazel@platige.com

http://www.azazel.carbonmade.com

BLAZ
PORENTA

blaz.porenta@gmail.com

http://blazporenta.blogspot.com/

BRADFORD
RIGNEY

bradfordrigney@gmail.com

http://cryptcrawler.deviantart.com/

BRUNO MELO
DE SOUZA

bmmsouza@gmail.com

http://bmelo.cgsociety.org/

CESAR
MARTINEZ ALVARO

kaesmartin@hotmail.com

http://kaesar30.cgsociety.org

CRAIG
SELLARS

sellarsart@hotmail.com

http://www.greensocksart.com

DAARKEN

daarkenart@daarken.com

http://www.daarken.com

DANIEL
LIESKE

daniel@digitaldecoy.de

http://www.digitaldecoy.de

DENIS
C. FELIZ

denisfeliz@gmail.com

http://www.denisfeliz.com.br

EDUARDO
PEÑA

caareka20@hotmail.com

http://chino-rino2.blogspot.com

FABRICIO
MORAES

fab.moraes@hotmail.com

http://fabmoraes.cgsociety.org

GERHARD
MOZSI

contact@gerhardmozsi.com

http://www.mozsi.com

http://www.mozsi.blogspot.com

GREGORY
CALLAHAN

sasquatchpoacher@gmail.com

http://gcallahan.com/

HAO AI
QIANG

metalcraer@hotmail.com

http://www.sleep-m.com/silentart

IKER
CORTÁZAR

iker.cortazar@gmail.com

http://icb.cgsociety.org/gallery/

JAMES
PAICK

james@scribblepadstudios.com

http://www.scribblepadstudios.com

JELMER
BOSKMA

3d58jelmer@vfs.com

http://www.jelmerboskma.com

JONATHAN
SIMARD

capitaine_star@hotmail.com

http://joofdeath.com/

KEKAI
KOTAKI

kekai.k@gmail.com

http://www.kekaiart.com

LEONID
KOZIENKO

leo@leoartz.com

http://www.leoartz.com/

LOÏC E338
ZIMMERMANN

info@e338.com

http://www.e338.com

MACIEJ
KUCIARA

fajny@maciejkuciara.com

http://www.maciejkuciara.com

THE 2009 DIGITAL ART MASTERS

MARC
BRUNET
finalxii@msn.com

http://bluefley.cgsociety.org

MAREK
DENKO
marek.denko@gmail.com

http://marekdenko.net/

MAREK
OKOŃ
omen2501@gmail.com

http://omen2501.deviantart.com

MARTIN
CARLSSON
martincarlsson3d@hotmail.com

http://www.marro.se

MICHAL
KWOLEK
kreska90@o2.pl

http://www.kwolek.org

NICHOLAS
MILES
nicholasmiles@gmail.com

http://www.nicksdesk.co.uk

http://www.exula.co.uk

NYKOLAI
ALEKSANDER
x@admemento.com

http://www.admemento.com

PIOTR
LUZIŃSKI
info@vp-cg.com

http://www.vertexophobia.com

ROBERTO
F · CASTRO
contact@robertofc.com

http://www.robertofc.com

RUDOLF
HERCZOG
rudy@rochr.com

http://www.rochr.com

RYOHEI
HASE
ryohei_hase@f6.dion.ne.jp

http://www.ryoheihase.com

SAREL
THERON
sarel@sareltheron.com

http://www.sareltheron.com

SEBASTIEN
HAURE
stuzzifr@hotmail.com

http://stuzzi.free.fr

SÖNKE
MAETER
soenkem@gmx.de

http://www.visual-noise.org

STEFAN
MORRELL
3dsmorrell@gmail.com

http://stefan-morrell.cgsociety.org

THIBAUT
MILVILLE
thibautmilville@club-internet.fr

http://www.back-elite.fr

TILL
NOWAK
tn@framebox.com

http://www.framebox.com

TITUS
LUNTER
crahzz@gmail.com

http://www.crahzz.com

TOMÁŠ
KRÁL
Info@tomaskral.cz

http://www.tomaskral.cz

TOMÁŠ
MÜLLER
temujin@temujin.cz

http://www.temujin.cz

VIKTOR
FRETYÁN
radicjoe@yahoo.com

http://radicjoe.cgsociety.org

VIKTOR
TITOV
viktortitov@yahoo.com

http://www.hamsterfly.com

http://hamsterfly.cgsociety.org

WEIYE
YIN
francwork@163.com

http://franccg.51.net

INDEX

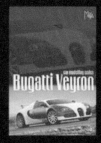

Printed and bound by CPI Group (UK) Ltd, Croydon, CR0 4YY

21/10/2024

01777096-0020